Among Penguins

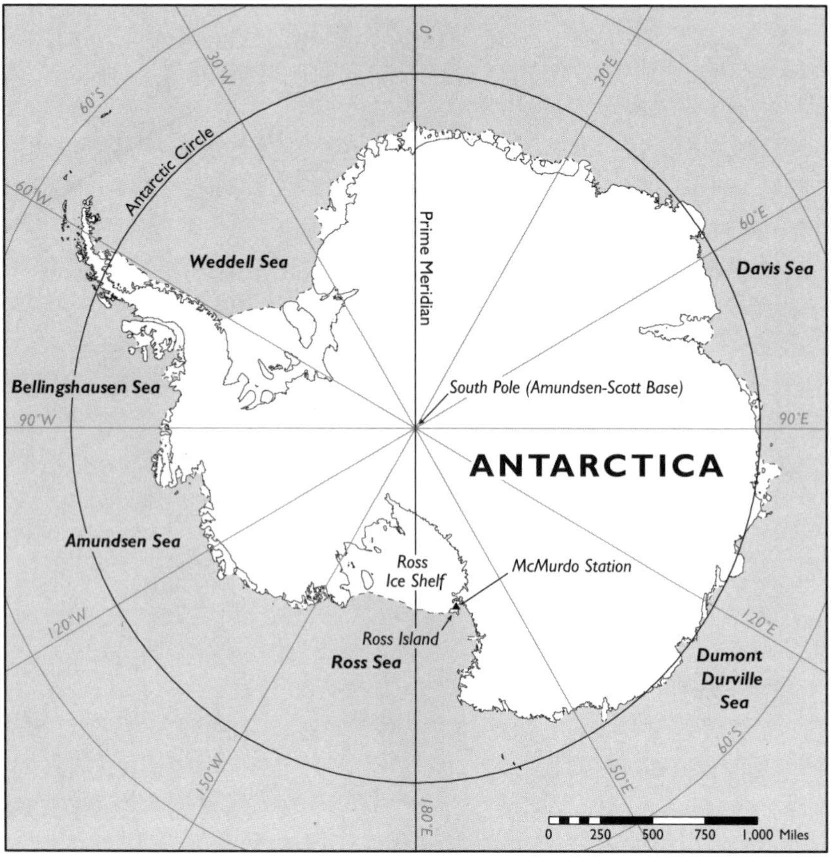
0°
30°W
30°E
60°S
60°W
60°E
Antarctic Circle
Prime Meridian
Weddell Sea
Davis Sea
Bellingshausen Sea
South Pole (Amundsen-Scott Base)
90°W
90°E
ANTARCTICA
Amundsen Sea
Ross
Ice Shelf
McMurdo Station
120°W
120°E
Ross Island
Ross Sea
Dumont
Durville
Sea
150°W
150°E
180°E
0 250 500 750 1,000 Miles

Map by Grace Gardner

The John and Shirley Byrne Fund for Books on Nature and the Environment provides generous support that helps make publication of this and other Oregon State University Press books possible. The Press is grateful for this support.

PREVIOUSLY PUBLISHED WITH THE SUPPORT OF THIS FUND:

One City's Wilderness: Portland's Forest Park

by Marcy Cottrell Houle

Among Penguins
A Bird Man in Antarctica

Noah Strycker

Oregon State University Press
Corvallis

The paper in this book meets the guidelines for permanence and durability of the Committee on Production Guidelines for Book Longevity of the Council on Library Resources and the minimum requirements of the American National Standard for Permanence of Paper for Printed Library Materials Z39.48-1984.

Library of Congress Cataloging-in-Publication Data
Strycker, Noah K.
  Among penguins : a bird man in Antarctica / Noah K. Strycker.
    p. cm.
  Includes index.
  ISBN 978-0-87071-629-4 (alk. paper)
  1. Penguins--Behavior--Antarctica. I. Title.
  QL696.S473S79 2011
  598.4709989--dc22

                        2010049245

First published in 2011 by Oregon State University Press
Printed in the United States of America

Oregon State University Press
121 The Valley Library
Corvallis OR 97331-4501
541-737-3166 • fax 541-737-3170
http://oregonstate.edu/dept/press

Table of Contents

1. Whiteout

❄❄❄

Kirsten, Michelle, and I leaned over the digital weather display as all hell broke loose.

"Seventy-five!" I gloated. An invisible freight train rammed the side of our tiny Antarctic hut, shaking the building to its icy foundations.

"Feels like we're about ready for liftoff," Kirsten said. She was resting in a metal folding chair, arms loose on the plastic table, which was elegantly crammed between reinforced bunk beds and a propane stove. With long fair hair, an athletic build, and a no-nonsense approach to rugged conditions, Kirsten Lindquist was tougher than most young women, was nicer than most tough chicks, and knew more about penguins than most other blonde Californians, except maybe the one sitting adjacent.

"We've got a blizzard on our hands, all right," agreed Michelle from the next chair over. Slim and strong, with wisps of blonde falling from under a soft hat, Michelle Hester commanded this tiny field station. Right now she was reclining in stripped-down cold-weather gear, finishing a delicious pancake breakfast.

The famous Antarctic wind was kicking into action. All morning, it had not dropped below fifty miles per hour, and each gust peaked a little higher than the last. Penguins and humans were in for a real storm.

I scanned the display as I munched a frozen Hershey's bar. "Fifteen below," I remarked, unimpressed. "Wonder what the wind chill is?" Flipping a couple buttons on the weather computer gave a quick answer. The effective air temperature, with wind factored in, was close to forty degrees below zero. It wasn't worth thinking too hard about.

"Eighty!" interrupted Michelle.

Our field hut, the size of a double-wide restroom, rocked and shuddered in the onslaught. Though the tiny structure was permafrosted to its foundation, and had already withstood a couple decades of Antarctic storms (with windblown stones embedded in the south wall to prove it), this was a bit unnerving.

I thawed my mouthful of chocolate, and continued to stare at the numerals measuring wind speed. Kirsten, Michelle, and I, sitting in front of the display, could not tear our eyes away. The weather monitor was hypnotizing, transfixing—better than television, even if we had a TV. It was like staring into a fire.

Michelle ate her pancakes thoughtfully. As an established biologist and ecologist, she could reflect on an accumulating stack of conservation credentials in far-flung areas, including tracking albatrosses in the Pacific, documenting exotic species in the Lesser Antilles, and, perhaps closest to her heart, overseeing Oikonos, a nonprofit organization dedicated to understanding and preserving ecosystems in a variety of landscapes. She'd been to Antarctica before, and lived in this same hut in prior seasons.

"One time," Michelle said, "I was trapped in here for forty-eight hours straight while the wind did not dip below a hundred. In that storm, we recorded a peak gust of a hundred forty-two miles per hour. That was crazy. We had to use a chamber pot because it was too dangerous to go outside to reach the outhouse."

She lifted a strand of hair over her ear, staring at the weather monitor. Michelle was a veteran here while I was a newcomer in my first field season. I struggled to comprehend such a blizzard. Holy crap, it must have been insane. If the wind was battering us now, just imagine a gust twice that strong.

In distraction, I bit a too-hasty chunk of Hershey's. Ouch. The frozen bar broke into dangerously pointy shards, and one piece pricked the roof of my mouth. In Antarctica, we consumed chocolate the way porcupines mate—very carefully. I delicately probed the sore spot with my tongue.

Outside, the wind roared.

A thirty-mile-per-hour gust might force a stutter-step as you walk normally. At fifty, you can lean into the wind, and at seventy-three miles per hour the storm officially becomes a hurricane. Around a hundred, you can't stand up without holding on to something solid. Closer to a hundred fifty, the wind might actually pick you up and blow you away.

I pulled my gaze from the weather computer and glanced out our tiny window. Things looked pretty fierce outside—the wind was kicking up snow crystals, and a whiteout seemed imminent. Flying snow already blotted out the sun, casting a gray gloom.

We were caged inside the hut. It was too dangerous to venture down to the penguin colony.

"Wonder how the penguins are doing," I mused aloud.

"They're fine," said Kirsten, shifting positions on the squeaky metal folding chair. "Penguins are made for this stuff." Kirsten, like Michelle, was used to tough field conditions, as evidenced by several trips to survey seabirds from commercial ships in the north Pacific, in between banding songbirds at Point Reyes Bird Observatory near San Francisco. She had also spent a previous season in Antarctica, doing her job with such capable assurance that project leaders invited her back for another round of penguin studies. Inside the hut, she had stripped to fuzzy mid layers, hanging her bulky jacket and wind pants neatly on a hook. She wore a typical hint of a smile.

"Yeah," agreed Michelle, "they hunker on their nests, streamline their bodies to the wind, and ride things out."

"They must really hate this weather, though," I said.

Michelle took another bite of pancake. "The only issue is that when enough snowdrifts pile up, penguins can get buried as they incubate eggs. They won't leave their nest, and, in the worst storms, a few sometimes suffocate. But I wouldn't worry too much about penguins—for them, this is home. They're pretty tough."

The three of us regarded each other at point-blank range inside our nine-by-fifteen-foot indoor space, thinking about the birds

9

out in the blizzard. Less than a mile from our hut, more than a quarter-million Adélie Penguins were enduring the unchecked storm. I shivered involuntarily. Even if they were accustomed to being out in bad weather, could they really enjoy it? I tried to picture all those penguins huddled in blinding snow. I, for one, was glad to have a propane heater and four sturdy walls.

"We just hit eighty-five!" Kirsten said.

Michelle's eyes flicked across the room to glance through a tiny, frosty window, and she looked suddenly nervous. "Better check on the tents," she said.

Conditions outside the window were approaching chaos. Two days before, several inches of fresh powder had accumulated in a rare snowfall. Now, all that loose snow was airborne. Driving winds lifted it right off the ground. The effect resembled something between an Afghan sandstorm and the interior of a ping-pong ball. Energy and motion overwhelmed the senses, and visibility dropped to just a few feet. Inside the storm, day turned to evening.

A couple of yellow tents were barely visible out in the gloom, providing the only color in a gray-and-white landscape. Fabric snapped hard as each gust slammed home, but the tents were holding up—so far. Scott tents, specially designed for Antarctic expeditions, are made of a welded aluminum frame draped with two heavy layers of cloth and an entrance tunnel. They are rated to eighty-mile-per-hour winds; anything beyond that is dangerous territory.

Though unheated and relatively exposed, the tents afforded a measure of privacy, so each of us had our own to sleep in. After all, we three were crammed together here, isolated from civilization, for three months. We got along very well, but everyone needs some room to stretch out.

"We should probably check the ropes," Kirsten said.

Michelle and I nodded. Each tent was tethered, held by rocks, and frozen to the ground, but the tethers could always bear tightening, especially the top ropes.

"Let's go before this gets any worse," Michelle said. She quickly wiped her plate with a paper towel and began pulling on layers of clothing. Kirsten and I followed suit. Inside the hut, the three of us had barely enough space to stand simultaneously, and getting dressed required coordination. My half-eaten Hershey's bar rested on the table.

I was already wearing two pairs of long underwear, pants, synthetic socks, and two thermal shirts. On top of this, I added another heavy shirt, special wind pants, a bulky down jacket, balaclava, two pairs of gloves, a radio harness, and ski goggles. I slid my feet inside specialized white bunny boots, designed to insulate against extreme temperatures. Generally, Antarctica is only cold if you don't pile on enough layers—as the saying goes, there is no bad weather, only bad clothing. Dressing for the outdoors meant at least ten minutes of preparation. Inside the hut, the heater provided some comfort, but heading into the storm required full cold-weather gear.

Of course, penguins are always ready for the cold. Their plump bodies are covered with insulating blubber, like a whale's. Compared to them, my own insulation was virtually nonexistent; my lean body is more like an antelope than a penguin.

"Ready?" Kirsten asked, smiling.

"As ever," I muttered, fully prepared to face my first blizzard. I gripped the door handle firmly, turned it, and pushed outward, abandoning the safety of the hut, not quite expecting what came next.

The door almost ripped off its hinges. Wind caught the surface like a sail, and I just hung on, muscling into the raw elements. I gasped. The strong force and pressure of the air inhibited normal breathing, especially since it was so cold and dry. I was glad for the ski goggles. Sunglasses would have been whipped off my face. The hem and hood of my red parka attempted to lift me into the heavens, and I reflexed into an instinctive crouch. Talking was impossible, so Kirsten, Michelle, and I communicated mostly in gestures, pointing and nodding. We dropped to all fours and angled away from the hut, following a lifeline rope tied between the building and my sleeping tent a hundred yards downhill, slowly drifting into a murky, swirling, gray, exposed gloom.

I crawled with deliberate movements, gripping scattered volcanic rocks to avoid rolling and sliding off course. Each gain was hard fought. Snow and ice particles skidded through the air and chafed like sand on my exposed cheeks as I followed the dim outline of Michelle in front, working across the open space between the hut and my tent.

I wished I were a penguin. A penguin's low center of gravity and crampon-like toenails keep the bird planted firmly on ice. In this wind, we were being blown all over the place. It was impossible to stay steady without at least one hand touching the ice for support, and the general noise and motion made it hard to concentrate.

It's difficult to describe the interior of a subzero hurricane because the experience involves so much disorientation. Imagine standing on the roof of a car traveling a hundred miles per hour on the freeway, in a blizzard, while wearing twenty pounds of insulation, and you begin to get the idea.

As my tent emerged into view, we realized we were on a salvage mission. Michelle crawled up to the teepee-like canvas structure, trying to catch a breath on the lee side, but the shelter had collapsed and provided little respite from the blizzard. My $3,000 Scott tent was trashed. The power of driven air had almost completely flattened it. A three-foot-wide hole gaped in one side. Through this hole, twisted and jagged pieces of metal were visible. The inch-thick aluminum support poles had bent and snapped like toothpicks. Only a frozen ground cloth and rocked-in supports had kept the tent from being blown across limitless miles of barren ice into oblivion. I couldn't have inflicted the same damage myself. Where my head had been sleepily pillowed two hours before, metal and torn canvas heaved viciously.

In an instant, the wind smashed me off my feet. I avoided being shot like a wrecking ball through the tent's walls by grabbing for and desperately grasping a sharp rock, scrabbling for a stronger foothold. "Come on, is that all you've got?" I shouted. The wind swallowed my voice like a teardrop in a swimming pool.

Wind sounded a full broadside in my ears, whistling and roaring like a banshee. We secured the wreckage of my tent as best we could, but there wasn't much to be done apart from grabbing my sleeping pad and bag; the tethers and rocks were already taut. The structure just wasn't designed to take this kind of abuse.

Michelle and Kirsten, judging phase one of our mission complete, began to retrace their way along the life rope, navigating toward their own sleeping tents. I lingered for several moments in an enforced crouch next to my demolished tent and watched them pick their way carefully, buglike, across the rock and ice. Ferocious tendrils of snow crystals scudded along the ground like sand on an exposed beach, with the same erosive effect.

Hundred-mile-per-hour gusts whipped by. All I could do was flatten myself to the ice and wait for a lull. How did the penguins manage it? What kind of animal could thrive in these conditions? After all, this was a relatively minor storm. In winter, when the sun never rises above the horizon in Antarctica, blizzards could be fifty degrees colder. Few humans have ever visited this place in winter. Some of those who had made the journey were lucky to get out alive—others, not so fortunate. Meanwhile, penguins endure all seasons without a chink in their curious and engaging personalities.

Certainly, penguins would be out of place on the streets of a big city. In human civilization, thousands of miles away, they wouldn't be able to find fish, argue over nest stones, or nap on an ice floe. They'd wander among city traffic without a clue. Penguins couldn't be comfortable in our world, so why should we be comfortable in theirs? To seek and understand these birds, I had to leave one realm and enter another.

The storm raged, but I embraced it. After weeks of relatively benign conditions, I was at last experiencing life on the edge. With one double-gloved fist wrapped around a rock, I pumped

13

the other in the air. Shazam! This was it—fulfillment of a dream, risk and reward. Adversity and isolation were exalting. I wanted to capture this moment and paste it in a scrapbook.

Mostly, though, I wanted to feel like a penguin.

❋

The storm raged unabated for thirty-six hours. Michelle, Kirsten, and I sat pinned inside the hut, listening to the wind batter our walls and noting its force on the digital weather monitor. During the blizzard, the wind never slacked below sixty miles per hour and frequently spiked over a hundred. Stronger gusts shook us like an earthquake. The noise was incredible. Even within the tight confines of the hut, we shouted to each other to get words across. After the first day, I couldn't remember what silence was like. Reality had shifted to a continuously screaming, howling, rattling state. The elements were in motion, and we were along for the ride.

Initially, the three of us tried to get some work done in the enforced captivity of the storm. After several hours of entering data and cleaning the interior of the hut, we ran out of productive things to do. We divided our entertainment between watching the hypnotizing weather monitor display and the drama out the window, where a chaotic whiteout obscured most of the view. At times, we couldn't even see the large rock five feet past the window glass. Flying snow particles blotted out sun, ground, and everything in between. Light barely penetrated the gray gloom. To venture out would have been asking for serious trouble.

So we stayed barricaded inside, and fretted about the weather.

Whenever the whiteout thinned, we watched my Scott tent, visible a hundred yards outside the hut's window. I was fascinated by its destruction. With the wind blowing straight through, the tent's skeleton of solid welded aluminum pipe snapped. The entire structure had collapsed, flattened and completely wasted.

Since our hut window was small, set high over the narrow aisle between bunks, only one of us could spy on my tent at any given time. We rotated window positions, standing on tiptoe to elevate our chins over the sill, catching the action from the tiny indoor space.

I mourned the loss of my home. Kirsten's and Michelle's tents were invisible to us, since there were no windows on the windward side of the hut, where the glass would have been shattered. We later discovered that Michelle's tent also had been flattened, but Kirsten's had somehow survived the onslaught.

It was my turn to cook dinner. I seized the opportunity to spend extra time on a special meal, pouring my soul into a pot of delicious spaghetti, with a sauce packed full of tasty meats and veggies, sides of bread, and cheese. I even apportioned part of my personal spicy V8 to mix Bloody Marys. Salad, alas, was out of the question, since fresh produce was unattainable. We tried not to fantasize too much about iceberg lettuce.

The sizzling sauce and steamy, boiling noodles cheered our indoor setting considerably while the storm blasted outside. Soon, the three of us crouched around the tiny table, eating dinner together, as we did each evening. It was a familiar routine, except for the novel feeling of being inside a hurtling train.

"We'll have to order a helicopter to bring us at least one more tent," said Michelle, winding a long piece of spaghetti on her fork.

"Yeah," Kirsten said, "if this storm ever stops."

"Impossible to fly in these conditions," Michelle agreed.

"A helo would never even get off the ground!"

"Will they replace my tent?" I asked. "I mean, this hut is nice and cozy, but I do like my spot on the ice …"

"I think so," Michelle said. "It might take a few days, but we should get an emergency resupply flight from McMurdo for the damaged equipment."

"That means mail!" said Kirsten.

"And freshies," I agreed, dreaming of tomatoes.

"Assuming we can talk someone into sending some on the flight," Michelle corrected. "Not a given in any circumstances."

15

Kirsten smiled. "It'll sure be weird to have visitors out here. I've forgotten what it's like to socialize with more than two other people at once."

Ironically, the storm that so completely isolated us inside the hut would precipitate our next contact with the exterior, civilized world. Three days later, a helicopter would land with two new Scott tents, extra propane, a bit of mail, and—most important—a small box of fresh tomatoes and onions.

2. Why?

✳✳✳

Half of my friends were immediately envious when I landed a four-month penguin research internship in Antarctica.

"Hook me up," they joked. "Wish I could go. You know how much it costs to travel there as a tourist?"

It's true. Desire alone isn't enough to get you to Antarctica. Limited positions are available for a number of research projects at several stations on the ice. Otherwise, vacationers might pay upward of $25,000 for a single slot on a cruise ship to southerly oceans, hoping for a day or two on land while observing penguins from a strictly enforced distance. Not many folks get the opportunity to go one-on-a-quarter-million with an entire colony of penguins—and get paid for it.

My other friends weren't envious at all.

"Have fun in that wasteland," they smirked. "Sounds like a torture test. Hope you survive."

Many of them simply asked: "Why? Why would you ever want to go there?"

It's a good question. Antarctica is a barren, icy desert, not the kind of place that humans are adapted to hang out in. It's the windiest, coldest, driest, highest, least populated, and most remote continent. There are excellent reasons why, even today, nobody lives permanently in Antarctica. It's too extreme to support our life.

Every year, though, several thousand people from the other six continents venture south to conduct research, promote conservation, operate machinery, perform feats of endurance, create art projects, and even write books. For a few people, Antarctica represents the epitome of adventure, a place to relish being out of their element. Something in the soul yearns to go beyond the horizon.

One particular friend just couldn't grasp this wanderlust. As we warmed up on the Oregon State University (OSU) tennis courts one afternoon, he tried to wrap his mind around it.

"So, you're gonna be living in the middle of nowhere," he began.

"Yep," I replied.

"For three months."

"You got it."

"With just two other people."

"Right."

Thwock, thwock, thwock went the tennis ball, rallying between our rackets. The familiar rhythm of tennis relaxed me, as it had through four years of college matches. I'd miss tennis in Antarctica.

"And there's no way to shower, wash clothes, or talk on the phone."

"Correct!" I said, brightly.

He shook his head slowly. "And it's, like, twenty below all the time?"

"More or less," I agreed.

"Dude, are you kidding me?"

"Not in the slightest!"

"Just to hang out with some penguins? Why don't you go to the zoo?"

"Zoos are overrated," I replied.

That was the end of conversation, and we were soon locked in a close duel. While playing tennis, the world for me ends at the sidelines. Off-court, though, my mind was drifting farther and farther south, even as I prepared to hang up my rackets for a few months.

Fresh out of college, at twenty-two years old, my definite priority was to see the world. Few people have the chance to be simultaneously unattached, uncommitted, debt free, healthy, and full of energy. Whether by a job, family, health, or financial constraints, most people are firmly tied down, some more happily than others.

The more extreme, remote, and isolated a place is, the more I want to go there. The farther it is from everyday living, the better. Something about tough conditions makes me thrive.

Not that I'm running away from regular life. It's just that, for me, the essence of living is far from comfortable spheres of civilization. In the world's most remote places, life is lived on the edge, and, as such, is magnified. Nowhere could this be more true than on the frozen continent.

Still, I hadn't fully answered the most basic question. Why did I want to go to Antarctica? As I walked off the tennis court, covered in sweat, my thoughts were thousands of miles away.

At first, the answer seemed obvious.

Antarctica is awesome!

Antarctica is adventurous!

Antarctica has penguins!

Antarctica is the coolest place ever, even without the obvious pun!

The more I thought about it, the more the question forced me to look inward, define life goals, and figure out who I really wanted to be. The introspection was uncomfortable. For a long time I settled on a short answer, especially for doubters like my tennis opponent.

Why? 19

"Because I'm addicted to birds."

It was a good start.

3. South

❄❄❄

I had just graduated from the university, with a flexible outlook on employment, when I came across an enticing announcement: Adélie Penguin Population Ecology Internship. Why not? Antarctica sounded cool. Well, cold. And I liked wildlife and cold places. I corralled together some references, sent off an application, and figured that would be the last of it.

I knew it was a long shot. More than a hundred people applied.

A couple weeks later, my cell phone rang. It was Grant Ballard, a senior scientist at Point Reyes Bird Observatory and research biologist in Antarctica, who was in charge of hiring the Adélie project intern. I couldn't believe it—he was interviewing me for the job!

Hello, what size shoe do you wear? Do you have a Leatherman tool? Would you mind not taking a shower for three months?

Um, size nine—yeah I've got small feet but it's not true what they say—and consider the Leatherman mail ordered. Did you know it was invented and named by a guy who went to Oregon State? And, no, just so long as nobody else was bathing, either. I mean, showers aren't everything.

That was it. I was hired.

After pocketing the phone, I walked over to my wall calendar, drew a red line from November to February, and wrote ANTARCTICA across it in all-capital letters. At that moment, I was working in Hawaii, helping conserve endangered birds on the Big Island, and I struggled to reconcile that I'd soon be chilling with penguins on a big sheet of ice, where life was a hundred degrees colder. I stared at the calendar, flipped open to show a tropical beach. Antarctica seemed closer to the moon than to Hawaii.

As reality sank in, I became more and more excited. What a trip! Waltzing around with a bunch of penguins—it'd be like a show on the Discovery Channel! Something between *Ice Road Truckers* and *Planet Earth*, I mused, speed-dialing friends to brag about the new position.

Reactions were a bit reserved. Most of my friends were kicking classes in college or, like me, had recently graduated. Some of them just didn't seem to get it, at first. *You're going where, to do what?* Others were more enthusiastic, especially those who knew my penchant for remote places, and gave hearty congratulations and well wishes. Many felt compelled to give advice.

"Dude, no penguin raping," lectured my tennis partner's best friend, seriously. "Three months without girls, things could get tight—just don't take it out on the cute little animals—and, believe me, they'll all start to look pretty cute after a while ..."

I said I'd actually be living with two women and he momentarily brightened—"Dude!"—until I interjected that the other scientists were older and involved in serious relationships, and, unlike some people, I had more important things on my mind, like research (no, not that kind of research), and adventures (seriously, now), so the penguins, and the other scientists, were safe enough.

"Well, just be careful down there," he said, and muttered something about shrinkage.

Other advice proved more helpful.

"Don't get frostbite," expostulated my aunt. "I've seen that stuff on TV—you don't want it. Your toes fall off."

I promised that if frost tried to bite me, I'd break its jaw.

Several people independently ordered a souvenir, but not just any ordinary knickknack. "Don't forget to bring me back a penguin!" became the closing line of many conversations. Never mind the legal and ethical issues, or carry-on luggage restrictions. One young woman was more specific: "I want one that cuddles!"

Over the next weeks, I jumped through various hoops required by the U.S. Antarctic Program. I filled out enough paperwork to build a papier-mâché icebreaker ship. An intense physical

21

exam was also required, involving blood work, dental X-rays, immunizations, psychological assessments, and other tests. Little medical care is available in Antarctica, so any health problems could turn disastrous.

Completing the physical ahead of time in Hawaii proved a little tricky. A local dentist agreed to shoot an x-ray, even though I was not an official patient, if I never told anyone and paid cash in advance. For me, though, a lifelong hemophobe (ridiculously afraid of blood and needles), the medical exam was the biggest mental hurdle.

Four weeks before departure, I sprawled on the floor in a back room of the Hawaiian doctor's office, sweating profusely in the air-conditioned space. "Now, just relax," the doctor said. Nurses had spent the previous twenty minutes busily procuring a stretcher so I could lie flat on the floor for the blood test. "Let's see, where's the vein? Don't worry, this won't hurt a bit—"

I tried to think about roses and fluffy clouds, but my mind clamped on the needle stuck in my arm. My vision blurred, then went black. Sounds faded to an echo. My hands became numb. As consciousness dimmed, my body went into shock, convulsing on the stretcher.

I awoke thirty seconds later to several concerned faces peering down. "Don't worry," I croaked. "Happens every time."

Blood and needles have always bothered me. In fifth grade, I watched a kid slice his leg open on the swing set during recess and fainted at the gory sight, planted my face in the playground asphalt, and knocked out my front tooth. We rode to the emergency room together. A few years later, I conked during a high school sports physical, losing consciousness in the middle of the urine test, and woke up stretched out flat on the floor, pants around my ankles, with several nurses bending over me, gushing, "We heard a thunk in the bathroom!" Once, in the midst of a restaurant dinner, I scratched a mosquito bite, watched it bleed down my leg, and vomited over my plate—the waiter got an extra big tip for that meal. Another time, during a tennis match, the ball struck me in the glasses, slicing me over the eye, and, when I

predictably fainted, my panicked coach called an ambulance. And
… the list goes on. Anyway, I physically qualified. I was one step
closer to flying south.

I would be working in Antarctica for a research collaboration
called PenguinScience, involving Oregon State University,
Point Reyes Bird Observatory in California, and H. T. Harvey
& Associates, an ecological consulting firm. All U.S. presence
in Antarctica, however, is ultimately funded by the National
Science Foundation, as all projects there are rigorously scientific.
Everyone in Antarctica is either a scientist or works logistics
for the scientists. My employers emailed a packing list that
required some specialized shopping. In no particular order, it
advised mountaineering boots, hiking socks, synthetic underwear,
glacier glasses, ski goggles, waterproof gloves, max sunblock,
an ultralight swimmer's towel, laptop, headlamp, rechargeable
batteries, travel Scrabble, and high-quality chocolate, the last
of which could be used as currency in a Hershey's-dominated
marketplace. I added an assortment of DVDs and books, from
Horatio Hornblower to *French Verb Conjugation I*, and a pack of
biofriendly baby wipes. What else could a guy need?

When the pieces were gathered, my suitcases bulged. Little
space remained for Christmas presents from friends and family,
but I managed to add a few small packages, wrapped and
labeled *Do not open until December 25*. After departure in early
November, I'd essentially be cut off from mail service. It felt weird
to be planning holidays so far in advance, but the thought of a
guaranteed white Christmas brought a smile.

The days counted down. With two weeks to go, I spent a
sunny Hawaiian afternoon re-reading the ninety-four-page
U.S. Antarctic Program Participant Guide about "The Ice,"
as Antarctica is known to those who know, to make sure
nothing had been missed. The guide was packed with factoids
accompanied by photos of heavy machinery and people in cold-
looking situations.

Lounging under a palm tree, I studied faces in the photos.
Tough-looking men and a few women smiled out from under

23

thick red parkas and dark shades. I closed my eyes, squeezed my toes in the sand, and tried to imagine life at the end of the Earth.

Soon, I would be walking among penguins.

4. Arrival

❄❄❄

The Boeing C-17 Globemaster III U.S. Air Force cargo jet lacked
windows, so none of us in the cargo hold noticed we had touched
ice until the engines reversed to brake. Relieved smiles cracked
out all around. If a plane was going to crash in Antarctica, it
wouldn't be this one. Five hours after leaving New Zealand, ice
slid solidly under our tires.

I was seated among several dozen scientists, maintenance
workers, and administrative types in chairs that folded out from
the wall. Wires and switches sprouted from industrial-looking
gray surfaces inside the military plane's massive interior. The
ceiling loomed twenty-five feet high. Passengers shared the space
with piles of boxed mail, secured by cargo nets strapped to cleats
in the floor. Larger items, like a disembodied propeller and a
parked bulldozer, shifted back and forth with minor turbulence
under cinched straps. Still, plenty of floor space remained, and
several distinguished scientists passed the flight sacked out on
their fluffy Big Red down jackets.

Kirsten reclined with nodding chin against the plane's interior
wall, a pair of neon orange industrial noise-protection earmuffs
clamped over her ears. The headphones had been fitted and
drilled with iPod earbuds, a wire snaking into each side.

"Like a poor man's noise-canceling setup," Kirsten had
shouted at me earlier, over the din of barely insulated jets. "Works
better than the high-tech ones they sell in airplane catalogues,
and you could sit next to a jackhammer without worrying about
hearing loss."

Might as well be sitting next to a jackhammer, I grumbled,
trying to recall everything I'd ever read about hearing loss. Unlike
commercial airlines, this cargo jet's roar left nothing to the
imagination.

I'd spent the previous few days in Christchurch with Kirsten and Michelle before we headed to Antarctica and our field site at Cape Crozier. Michelle would follow on a later flight; Kirsten and I traveled south with Katie Dugger, a professor from OSU bound for a different penguin colony on Ross Island. She now sat with us. Katie, charmingly academic, had wrapped herself in her fluffy Big Red without wearing the sleeves, and I beckoned to her, motioning toward Kirsten. Katie grinned; even in sleep, Kirsten was actually smiling.

At touchdown, a brawny U.S. Air Force reservist, dressed in loose camo and a black Mountain Hardwear down vest, voiced his best flight attendant impression, speaking into an intercom. "Uh, folks, well, we made it. It's a beautiful, sunny day at McMurdo Station, light winds, about negative five degrees Fahrenheit. Try not to get sucked into the jets as you disembark."

He was from Washington State and worked in the Boeing factory near Seattle. He'd flown on cargo jets around the world and signed on the Antarctica transport mission, Operation Deep Freeze, as an interesting side trip. He hoped the plane would return to civilization without being stranded in sudden bad weather, which happened often enough that we all had packed special "boomerang" bags with an extra change of clothes in case the plane was forced to turn around mid-flight.

The reservist, with a salaried job and a family, was nervous about getting back home, halfway around the world. Earlier, in a slightly bored mid-flight conversation, he'd been eager to share his particular envy of the Special Ops guys, who carried laptops with handheld satellite Internet connections able to stay in constant contact with home. When I explained my relatively unattached life, he just grinned.

"Good luck out there, bro," he said, pounding knuckles, smoothing back a crewcut with one meaty hand. "Better you than me."

Here I sat, fresh out of college, wandering off to Antarctica to spend three months with penguins. I harbored no clear future plans, figuring opportunity could take care of itself. Later, sitting

alone in a freezing tent, I'd have more time to contemplate
the future. For now, I considered the obligations—mortgage,
kids, salary—pulling this Air Force guy in an entirely different
direction. We were about the same age, but literally flying on
different courses. I wouldn't have traded places for the world.

The cargo hold cooled to the temperature outside as we
descended, encouraging everyone aboard to suit up in their
special-issue extreme cold weather gear: "Big Red," a distinctive
U.S. Antarctic Program down jacket nicknamed for obvious
characteristics; black wind pants; white bunny boots; and ski
goggles. All U.S. Antarctic Program participants are assigned the
same twenty-two pounds of clothing in New Zealand, and are
required to carry it while traveling south. Everyone on the plane
wore exactly the same uniform. By the time we landed, the cargo
hold felt like a walk-in freezer, but my clothing was warm, and
all thoughts of temperature vanished as I shouldered my bags,
walked out into bright sunshine, tried not to get sucked into the
jets, and stepped onto the ice for the first time.

Antarctic winter is so cold that the ocean's surface freezes
fifteen feet thick, more than enough to support heavy aircraft
until the late summer melt. With a little grooming, the sea ice
provides a perfect runway most of the year.

Every now and then, penguins wander onto the runway and
must be ushered away so planes can land. Ever curious, the
penguins have been known to mingle in the beer parties of local
workers, standing around on the ice and staring at each other in
the low-angled sunshine of frigid summer evenings. None were in
sight this afternoon, though—beer parties or penguins.

Instead, Antarctica hit with an assaulting first impression.
The temperature registered several degrees below zero. The sun,
cutting through delphinium blue skies and slipping through a
large ozone hole, splashed brilliantly over the white, featureless
landscape. Even with darkened ski goggles, I squinted until my
eyes adjusted. Dry air, cold and crisp, sucked like chilled top-shelf
vodka into the lungs. I crunched in bunny boots over dry, packed
snow, and glanced around. But, besides people, no living thing

broke an endless expanse of icy white. All self-respecting penguins were miles away. Few deader-looking places exist on Earth.

The line of deplaning passengers looked inhuman as it moved onto the white expanse from the gray plane. Individuals seemed to act as robots in this landscape, coming to Antarctica with a work-oriented purpose, and caught in a system of mind-bending logistics. They formed abstract lines on the landscape, filing one after another and then breaking like water around an obstacle, regrouping into fiery swatches of startling American red colors. Already tugging at my mind was a sense of insignificance, but twenty-two-year-old adventurousness kept such thoughts suppressed. Once everyone had deplaned, passengers grouped together on the ice. I had trouble distinguishing folks without reading name tags among the Big Reds.

The scene reminded me of a now-yellowed cartoon I had stuck on my bulletin board at home. In a sea of huddled penguins, all exactly alike, one says to another, "Blind date? I don't know, what's she look like?"

Kirsten, Katie, and I moved toward a waiting vehicle and climbed inside, following the red tide, to be transported to McMurdo Station.

Our ride from the ice runway was a fifty-four-passenger, sixty-eight-thousand-pound beast with monster tires, named Ivan the Terrabus—a beloved McMurdo character. Manufactured by a Canadian company, Foremost, Ivan has been wheeling around on the ice for years, undaunted by storms and freezing weather. The bare metal interior is plastered with stickers placed by generations of Antarctic travelers: fire crews, army regiments, and musical groups have all left their marks inside.

Ivan (most people say *EYE-van* but I prefer the more exotic *eee-VAWN*) starred in a popular music video in the annual McMurdo Film Festival a couple months later, when an improbable tuba player backed up a guitarist who sang, "Ivan the Terrabus—he brings our friends to us!" over images of a rocket-fueled Ivan flying around the moon in a daydream. I wondered how the musicians had got a tuba to Antarctica.

For now, my own bulging luggage, barely within weight restrictions, zippered inside several orange cloth bags, was lost in a pile of identical bags with everyone else's stuff at the back of the terrabus. I didn't look forward to sorting it all out. Bag drag, the process of reclaiming and packing your luggage from place to place, is justifiably and universally dreaded at McMurdo Station. However, judging by all the grins behind goggles and hats, this busload was pretty psyched to be rolling into town. Ivan rumbled away from the airstrip across the miles of featureless ice, driving on the frozen surface of the ocean toward a collection of rugged mountains thrusting up through the icy plain. I stared out Ivan's thick windows, trying to angle a view of our destination, but the panes kept fogging with the collective breath from the inside. The condensation froze in place, obscuring the outdoors behind a white film. Not that it mattered much. The outdoors was white anyway.

I grinned under my Big Red's generous hood lining of real coyote fur, warmed by its insulation of Canada Goose feathers. Here I was chasing a dream, beginning a somewhat ambiguous lifestyle, unsure what would come next. Wherever my life led after college, it was starting in Antarctica. The thought of it was suddenly immensely satisfying. For me, the end of the world would dish out adventure—and provide a beginning.

Kirsten had packed away her headphones in favor of a fuzzy hat, and Katie sat with her hood pulled over sunglasses, bouncing gently with Ivan's scant suspension as we rolled over wind-carved ridges of packed ice. Looking around at the group inside the terrabus, I could see that we were entering a bundled-up existence. Once in our field camp, we'd be perpetually living in thick clothing without even the option of a shower. It was a claustrophobic thought.

First, though, before the penguins, before the isolation, the grime, the storms, and the months on ice, McMurdo Station loomed on the horizon—literally. I could just make out a ragtag collection of buildings through Ivan's frosty windows, as postcard-perfect as a Nevada mining camp.

5. McMurdo

As Ivan the Terrabus docked on the ice alongside Building 155 at McMurdo Station, an ambulance pulled in beside us. From my seat on the bus, I watched the medics through a frosty window.

Sunshine lit up the station, glaring off reflective surfaces and glinting on ice crystals. Frozen streets congealed with gravel, snow, and ice. Weather-worn exteriors looked shabby. Machinery lurked everywhere outside in parking spaces, alleyways, and empty lots: tracked Hagglund vehicles, monster Delta shuttles, Mattracked 4x4 pickups, bulldozers, tanks of oil and chemicals, ice drills, and industrial waste bins. Workers walked quickly between buildings, boots crunching on gravel, shoulders hunched into the crisp air. Such was life on the frontier.

Kirsten, from her seat in the back of Ivan's passenger space, leaned over and winked behind wraparound sunglasses.

"You know, if you smile any bigger, your head might split. But at least the hospital is right outside."

If I couldn't stop grinning, it wasn't my fault. I looked everywhere at once, snapping photos and soaking in first impressions of places and people. Antarctic veterans sat quietly, amused by the raw excitement of new recruits.

It would be a few days before we saw any penguins. The nearest colonies were miles away, and penguins rarely wandered past McMurdo. I had a week to chill in relative civilization before catching a helicopter to Cape Crozier, the penguin metropolis where I would be living and working for the season with Kirsten and Michelle.

Meanwhile, McMurdo Station presented an odd place to spend time.

The station itself is unusual. And everyone in it—up to fifteen hundred people in summer, forming the biggest "city" in Antarctica—must also be a little strange. The people, personalities, and culture among McMurdo's eccentric population add to its outcast environment.

The station is not by any means a diverse place. There are no kids, no old people, and no permanent residents. Men form two-thirds of the population. All are Americans, and less than 10 percent are minorities. However, on an individual level, everyone is unique. Ordinary people generally don't apply for jobs in Antarctica.

Werner Herzog's 2007 documentary *Encounters at the End of the World* was filmed here, and portrays Antarctica's most ingrained characters in a no-holds-barred, often unflattering (but mostly accurate) context. Probably for that reason, Herzog is viewed with suspicion or openly disliked by many who met him down south. Still, *Encounters* is an entertaining movie—totally Netflix it—and captures the eccentricity of life on The Ice.

I watched medics carry someone on a stretcher from the ambulance into an adjacent building, next to a hand-painted sign: "General Hospital." They disappeared inside, shutting the door quickly against the cold. Whoever was on the stretcher, bundled up, wasn't moving.

I was surprised to see a genuine ambulance here, red emergency lights flashing, thousands of miles from the nearest paved road. Later, I found out that the victim on the stretcher had been evacuated from the Amundsen-Scott South Pole Station with extreme altitude sickness. The pole sits on a thick ice sheet about ten thousand feet above sea level, and some visitors can't deal with such elevation. Their lungs fill with fluid, their brains swell, their doctors talk about edemas, and, unless the victims get to lower altitude, they die.

Building 155's coat room was like something from a practical joke. Hundreds of identical Big Reds aligned on coat hooks around the entryway's perimeter, two or three deep. A couple

31

guys had clearly forgotten where they had left their own assigned jackets, and were anxiously pawing through them all, one by one, reading name tags. I made a careful note of my chosen hook.

Adjacent rooms formed the center of McMurdo activity and organization. Building 155 held the store, kitchens, bank (including ATM), offices, and dorm rooms. Inside, the structure defied all expectations of stark functionality. A large cafeteria was furnished in sharp contrast to McMurdo's industrial exterior. Tasteful artwork decorated the walls, soft carpet padded underfoot, and comfortable furniture was arranged around tables. Against one wall, a bank of soda and juice machines dispensed unlimited refreshment. Like a few remote stations I'd visited in other parts of the world, McMurdo was outfitted with civilized accents.

I found an unoccupied table with Kirsten and Katie under a giant artistically framed picture of an Emperor Penguin, darting occasional glances toward the windows, still openly amazed by the environment.

Inside the heated, cozy cafeteria, it was easy to forget the brutal elements outside.

Orientation speeches were brief, covering weather, logistics, and living arrangements. An energetic doctor gave practical advice on staying healthy. "It may seem trivial, but wash your hands before you eat. Every year, germs pile up in McMurdo Station and eventually fuse into The Crud, a combination of flu, cold, and general disease. Most people catch it sooner or later." He made nasty gestures to illustrate his points. "And, speaking of eating, don't eat too much. Most people actually gain weight in Antarctica. The cafeteria serves four meals a day with an unlimited buffet. That Frosty Boy"—he glowered at an ice cream machine next to the juice dispenser—"is particularly deadly. Watch your portions. But you better eat everything on your plate. All that food had to be shipped halfway around the world."

Not just the food, I reflected. Everything at McMurdo Station, from building materials to postcards, was imported. And all waste had to be exported. More on that later.

"Antarctic life tends to magnify relationships. Keep that in mind. If your head gets twisted up, we offer counseling services, too. And there are condoms in the restrooms. Use 'em."

Sniggers from the peanut gallery.

The doctor ignored them. "Seriously, don't wander off-trail outside base. We are surrounded by dangerous ice. People have died falling into crevasses and over cliffs within sight of this building. If weather turns Condition One, you must stay inside until the storm breaks. In high winds, it's possible to step outside and not be able to get back in. Finally, have fun! You're in an extreme environment. Make the most of it. Take every opportunity. If you live through it, you'll be telling your grandkids about Antarctica."

As each orientation speaker talked, I glanced around the room at the dozens who had arrived on my flight. I felt aloof. Most of these people would spend the full summer season at McMurdo Station working in a wide range of jobs, from cooks and janitors to construction, communications, helicopter operations, and special projects. They'd settle in, form communities, develop an isolated culture, and live a crazy sort of city life until their terms were up.

For me, McMurdo was transitory. I'd spend a stressful week here, helping sort and pack gear, before flying out to my penguin field camp. While others decorated their dorm rooms and attended icebreakers (parties, not ships), I would work in the lab or run down equipment. But I counted myself lucky. Many people who visited McMurdo Station would never see a single penguin. Most of them envied my position. My job, after all, was the best in the world.

Kirsten and Katie had been booked in together, but I looked forward to a randomly assigned roommate for the week. So, after our orientation, we split up and I dropped by the housing office (behind the coat room, across the hall from the bank), picked up linens, and headed to my dorm to settle in. Moving between buildings required a trip outside, where trucks and bulldozers drove up and down dirty streets. While I clutched a giant roll

33

of bedding, a pickup passed in a cold cloud of dust and I did a double take on the license plate. It definitely said Idaho.

It took a while for me to figure out that McMurdo's fleet of battered red pickup trucks is stranded. The roads at McMurdo don't connect anywhere very far. One gravel thoroughfare leads to Scott Base, New Zealand's Antarctic station, a couple miles away. And ice roads extend to airfields on the ice shelf. Otherwise, you need a snowmobile, tracked vehicle, or alternate transportation to travel. Over the years, workers have affixed a diverse array of old license plates to the pickup trucks, representing several states.

As the dust settled, I noticed a metal door on an adjacent building, unremarkable except for a cryptic, carefully stenciled inscription. Someone had found time to mark a territory here in painted block capitals: "You Melta My Ice, I Breaka You Face."

❄

As I walked into my dorm room, my roommate extended a steady hand. "Hi, I'm David. Just arrived?"

In the tiny, cave-like room, the window shades had been pulled tight, presumably to encourage sleeping in an artificially darkened environment. Where the sun never sets for the whole summer, darkness is precious.

David was squat, baldish, and friendly. I asked what brought him to the frozen continent.

"Oh, playing with balloons. Actually, one really big balloon. And trying to find neutrinos." He must have spotted my quizzical look because he sat down, took a deep breath, and launched into an explanation. "OK, so there's this tiny particle that basically has no mass or charge, travels close to the speed of light, and passes through most material undetected. It's called a neutrino. Right?"

I nodded, as if I knew anything about physics, and sized up the dorm room while I listened. This place was just like college.

"My team is trying to study these particles. So we floated a huge balloon with detection equipment in the upper atmosphere above Antarctica. Think about how a telescope works: it gathers light through a large lens and channels it toward your eye. Well, our balloon works the same way. The sensors on our balloon form the eye, and the white reflective surface of the entire continent of Antarctica is the giant lens."

I tried to look impressed.

"My job," David continued, warming to his subject, "is to install a remote station up on the ice sheet that emits known neutrino particles, so we can see if the sensors on the balloon pick them up. It's a test to make sure the detection equipment works."

Suddenly, he leaned forward, and, in a serious tone, practically whispered: "Neutrino particles relate to dark matter. And dark matter relates to other dimensions of space that haven't yet been proven to exist!"

My roommate was studying unknown dimensions of space. Either he was really smart or a little crazy. Or both. But I gave him credit. Advanced Placement Physics class during senior year of high school was as far as I ever got, and I had been glad to pass the final exam.

David asked what I was in for, and I briefly explained the penguin project.

"Aha! Penguins. That makes you the Bird Man of Antarctica." The nickname fit well enough.

"Well, there's beer in the fridge, Bird Man. Help yourself. Some guy left it there before you got here. And welcome to The Ice."

I unpacked and stretched the linens on my bed. Every time I touched the mattress and floor carpet at the same time, static electricity sparked painfully in the extremely dry air.

Dorm rooms, new friends, cafeteria meals, orientation speeches. It all seemed unexpectedly familiar, like the first day at school. Hadn't I just graduated from school for, like, forever? I had the distinct impression of McMurdo Station as a summer camp for grownups. All it needed was an outdoor survival exercise—and that was coming.

I shouldn't have been surprised that the station hosts three separate bars: Southern Exposure (the smoking bar), Gallagher's (the nonsmoking bar), and the Coffee House (which serves wine), in order of descending bawdiness. I had an imminent dinner date with the penguin team at the last of these, and set off, throwing a salute to David on the way out. He was bent over the mini-fridge, either organizing beer or shoving it to the back to make space for something else, but glanced up in time to solidify my nickname.

"See you, Bird Man!"

6. Coffee House

The Coffee House used to be the officers' club, back when McMurdo Station served as a U.S. Navy base. Now, it's a quiet place, with subtle pop rock playing to a backdrop of vintage skis and sleds hanging on lacquered walls. In the T-shaped, windowless Quonset hut, the atmosphere is soothingly dark, giving the illusion of evening. People murmur around tables, sip wine and coffee, and act civilized. It's a good place to feel like an underachiever. Most of the clientele have climbed Everest, been knighted, discovered something new to science, or run naked across the Gobi Desert. You know the type, the people you read about in magazines.

David Ainley, the well-respected king of penguins, fit right in. I found him nursing a glass of wine at a corner table.

Gray-haired and mustached, Ainley may know more about penguins than anyone. He's been studying them in Antarctica for the past thirty years, publishing books and articles, and building a deserved reputation as the penguin man. Along the way, he developed the PenguinScience project, which now encompasses several study sites at different colonies around the Ross Sea. I'd be working at one of these sites, Cape Crozier, while he would spend the season at a separate penguin colony, Cape Royds. The only time we overlapped would be during gear-up in McMurdo.

I slid into an adjacent chair and introduced myself. Ainley's eyes showed quiet intelligence. His sentences were interspersed with thoughtful silences, unconcerned with keeping up conversation, but his words commanded attention. Every so often, someone would stop by our table and say hi, paying their respects to the great scientist. He held court at peace, stroking a snowy white mustache, nodding and shaking hands throughout the evening, sipping his wine, thinking about penguins.

Kirsten arrived, then Michelle, who had touched down on a later flight. Though we'd already spent a few days together in New Zealand, I was especially keen to get to know them both, as we'd be essentially locked up together, in cramped conditions, for months.

I needn't have worried. Michelle and Kirsten effused friendliness and competence. They'd both spent prior seasons working with penguins at Crozier.

"Shouldn't have had that extra Frosty Boy," Kirsten moaned.

"A Frosty Boy a day keeps the doctor away," chuckled Michelle.

"Tuck in to that ice cream while you can," advised David. "Pretty soon you'll be eating snow instead."

"Hey, chipped blue ice makes a great margarita," said Michelle.

"Did you hear about the group that received a Christmas box labeled as cooking oil?" asked Kirsten. "Customs didn't even open it!"

"Good idea," I mused. The single McMurdo Station store imposed strict limits on the amount of alcohol one could buy on any given day, and its selection was limited.

Conversation turned toward the future.

"Tomorrow morning, before we go, we should all hike up Obs Hill," Kirsten suggested.

"I'm game," said Michelle. "Got to balance out that Frosty Boy somehow."

Observation Hill, overlooking McMurdo Station from a height of about one thousand feet, offers a twenty-minute hard scramble up rocky trail and snow patches behind the maintenance buildings. At the summit, a weathered wooden cross memorializes Robert Scott and others who perished on the British South Pole expedition around 1910.

"The view from Obs Hill is almost as good as Pat's Peak, where we do whale watches at Crozier," Kirsten said.

"If you can mind the cold," Ainley added. "Nothing compares to the view of a quarter-million penguins spread out below you."

The anticipation was almost unbearable.

"Cheers to that!" I said, raising my glass of wine.

"To a great season," agreed David.

"Agreed," chimed in Kirsten.

"And good weather," said Michelle.

"Well, with one or two good storms for the record," I winked.

We talked late, over bottles of wine and appetizers, with the singular enthusiasm of expectation: planning, scheming, worrying, and wondering what awaited us in the months ahead. Eventually, I said goodbye to Ainley. We'd meet up back at McMurdo three months later for the return U.S. flight. He wished Michelle, Kirsten, and me luck.

When I finally stumbled off to my dorm room, it was 1 a.m. On the streets of McMurdo Station, the sun shone at a low angle, helicopters chopped overhead like giant insects, and a chilly breeze blew. Loud bass thumped from Southern Exposure and Gallagher's, both a hundred yards from the Coffee House. Several New Zealanders in black-and-orange jackets were loitering, gloved hands in pockets, waiting for a shuttle to take them back over the hill to Scott Base. American workers on the night shift had just finished eating lunch, a midnight meal in the cafeteria called midrats, and were walking to jobs in other buildings.

Geographical outposts the world over give out the same grungy, wayward, almost-forgotten vibe. This one carried an undercurrent of raw energy.

7. A Very Brief History of Penguins

❄❄❄

Antarctica is a continent, not a country. It's one and a half times as big as the U.S., and 98 percent of the land is covered by a permanent ice sheet up to three miles thick. No nation really owns any part of Antarctica, though a few countries stake territory in various areas. Big chunks aren't yet claimed by anyone, the only free land left on Earth (the North Pole, remember, doesn't have solid land under its ice).

The entire human population of Antarctica is about five thousand in summer and one thousand in winter. Compare that to the U.S., which has a much smaller landmass, but more than three hundred million residents. You could gather all the people in Antarctica during its busiest season, ask each of them to invite several friends, and easily seat the entire party inside Yankee Stadium (or Fenway Park). Not that baseball is relevant, except that Antarctica is a sparse place for a social life.

But the empty land holds thriving cities.

Its greatest metropolises are inhabited by penguins. About five million Adélie Penguins and several hundred thousand Emperor Penguins occupy Antarctica. That's more than a thousand penguins to every human. Like people, they live in dense colonies, mostly clustered around coastlines, though the penguin cities and human stations are often in different places since today's explorers try not to impose on the wildlife.

People used to call penguin cities rookeries, but, these days, that term is uncool, relegated to other birds like herons and egrets. Now, scientists prefer the more anthropomorphic term, colony, to describe an outpost of civilization. Penguin colonies are scattered around the margins of Antarctica, in places with exposed rocks, access to open ocean, and enough fish and krill to eat. People need the same things—shelter, space, and food—and, like penguins, many humans live near a coast. We are quite alike when it comes to basic arrangements.

Today, there are more than one hundred and sixty Adélie Penguin colonies distributed on Antarctica and its offshore islands, with stable or increasing populations. Numbers of Emperor Penguins declined by half in the past fifty years at the Pt. Geologie colony, and the colony at Dion Islet has disappeared, but scientists don't know whether other Emperor colonies are increasing or decreasing. Modern snapshots aside, we are now seeing the result of eons of change on a grand scale. The land and birds have had a long history.

At one time, Antarctica was tropical, with warm temperatures, in an age with four times the modern atmospheric carbon dioxide. About two hundred million years ago, it was connected to the other continents in one burly hunk we call Gondwanaland. Antarctica nurtured trees and large animals, including dinosaurs, whose fossilized remains are now being carted off by adventurous paleontologists in Big Red jackets and snow goggles. But penguins evolved more recently.

About forty million years ago, gigantic penguins appeared in Antarctica. They were six feet tall and weighed close to two hundred pounds—the kind of bird you wouldn't want to meet in a dark alley. As eons progressed, those giants went the way of the dinosaurs, leaving smaller lineages that evolved into modern penguins.

DNA evidence suggests that Adélies diverged genetically from other species about twenty million years ago, after Antarctica split with South America. Since then, the region has seen some major climate shifts. Antarctica's land has been covered in ice for the past few million years, as ocean currents changed and the continent settled over the South Pole, cooling dramatically. Penguins have dealt with ice ages every hundred thousand years or so, with dramatic fluctuations in sea level, gradually adapting and evolving over time.

41

Then people came along.

Portuguese sailors may have encountered South African Jackass Penguins in the late 1400s, but Ferdinand Magellan gets credit for "discovering" and documenting the first true penguins around 1500. The Magellanic Penguin was named after him, and it lives to this day, oddly enough, in the Straits of Magellan. Antarctic penguins, though, would have to wait a couple hundred more years to meet a human.

Around 1830, a French naval officer named Jules Sébastien César Dumont d'Urville, on an expedition to Antarctica, apparently decided to classify the small, friendly penguins that his sailors were clubbing over the head. With dashingly romantic French spirit, and maybe because his own name was just too long, he christened the birds after his wife, Adélie. Twelve years later, Dumont and his family burned to death in a fiery train crash near Versailles on their way to Paris, an ironic demise for the Antarctic explorer. Adélie never actually saw a penguin, but her name stuck, and explains the Frenchy accent on the first "é."

Speaking of names, nobody is quite sure where the word penguin originated. The Latin term *pinguis* roughly translates to fat, oily, sleek, rich, and fertile—all of which might describe a penguin. On the other hand, the Welsh words *pen* and *gwyn* together mean "white head." Most penguins don't have white heads (they're black), but their seabird relative of the north seas, the now-extinct Great Auk, which might have been eaten in Wales, had a partly white head in winter. Maybe the name got transposed somewhere.

Early on, names were less important than what they represented. Penguins meant food for Antarctic explorers, supplementing a lean caloric intake. The birds were easy to catch because they had no fear of humans. One good whack over the head, and fresh meat was on the table, or ice block. The trouble was, an average eight-pound Adélie didn't have much flesh on its body and it tasted horrible. Seals provided a better food source.

I've never partaken of penguin (though I have eaten other birds, including parrots and trogons), and, from descriptions of

42

its flavor and texture, I probably never will. The meat has been compared to that of gulls and pelicans—although, since most people haven't eaten one of those, either, that doesn't say much. Generally, birds that consume fish and seafood taste the worst, surpassed only by carrion eaters like vultures. So, penguins, with an entirely fishy diet, would be expected to taste pretty bad. Accordingly, a chef once suggested you could mimic a penguin's flavor by binding chicken breast between two spruce boards, boiling it in crude oil and diesel, then throwing away the chicken and eating the boards. Between penguins and pemmican, early Antarctic explorers had a rough diet.

These days, the only ones eating penguins are Leopard Seals. The birds, along with all of Antarctica's wildlife, are strictly protected by the Antarctic Treaty and specific conservation laws. Most people aren't even allowed to approach a penguin without specialized permits. They're as sacred as cows in India.

OK, maybe not quite sacred. Penguins, probably owing to their remote range, don't figure prominently in world religions. However, they are so universally appealing that penguins have become an icon in modern pop culture. The birds have reached a cliché of well-mannered, exotic, and slightly nerdy allure.

For instance, a recent question posed on Yahoo! Answers asked:

"If a kindly penguin asked you for a Marlboro, would you give her one?"

Dozens of readers crafted hypothetical replies. Most agreed they would be happy to lend the penguin a cigarette:

"Of course—anything to corrupt a penguin."

"I would say, 'Wow! A talking penguin!' And ask if she liked Menthol."

"I'd hook her up with a lifetime supply!"

Only one respondent was immune to the siren call of the penguin:

"No," he replied. "I don't smoke, and penguins shouldn't either."

Enough said.

In the past century, casual onlookers have been able to enjoy real penguins at zoos, thanks to the wonders of modern transportation, refrigeration, and housing systems. Edinburgh Zoo received three King Penguins in 1914, the first to be held in captivity for public scrutiny. Since then, the zoo collection has expanded, and one of Edinburgh's penguins even received a knighthood in 2008 from the King of Norway in a complex ceremony involving speeches, medals, and thirty members of the Norwegian Guard.

In the U.S., few places are less hospitable to penguins than the arid deserts of southern Nevada. However, at the Flamingo Las Vegas, a giant casino-resort on the shimmering, glitzy Strip, distracted gamblers can linger—drinks in hand—to watch Jackass Penguins cavort among Chilean Flamingos and other exotic birds in a luxurious garden a stone's throw from the poker tables. We've come a long way since Portuguese sailors first encountered Jackass Penguins in South Africa in the late 1400s. Today, more tourists drool over them in Las Vegas than in the wild.

But—hold on a sec! If more people watch penguins in captivity than in the wild, what do we really think of these birds? Pop culture and zoos have ripped penguins out of context faster than you could shred the latest copy of the *Enquirer*. We've assigned stereotypes and reduced penguins to simple, accessible characters. In modern society, they are increasingly disconnected from wild environments.

Watching a penguin in captivity couldn't compare to experiencing one on its home turf, if turf existed in Antarctica. Though penguins are charming on their own, it's their rugged habitat that gives them such exotic appeal. No concrete rocks or plastic icebergs could ever approach the real thing, millions of years in the making. For the real deal, you've got to seek penguins on their own terms.

8. Ice Figure

❄❄❄

Michelle and Kirsten were working hard, running errands all over McMurdo Station to prepare for our penguin field camp at Cape Crozier. They had to plan everything for three self-sustaining months on the ice—from tents, propane, and food to satellite tags and communications gear. The logistics were mind boggling.

Michelle, who would head the field station, set up a complicated whiteboard in our temporarily assigned lab to delineate tasks, provide checklists, and hash out a schedule. I was surprised to find that helicopter trips were scheduled and grocery orders placed mere days in advance. In the face of Antarctica's unpredictable weather, planning far ahead didn't always make sense. Each morning the penguin team held a conference to figure out priorities.

I helped wrangle equipment, but survival took official priority. Since this was my first trip south, protocol dictated two full days of outdoor training exercises involving sea ice safety and emergency camp preparation. So, with a stacked week to look forward to, I said my temporary goodbyes to Michelle and Kirsten, packed a bag of extra clothing, bundled into Ivan the Terrabus with a busload of strangers, and drove into the white expanse of the Ross Sea.

Less than a day after arriving in Antarctica, I found my feet firmly planted on the ice, a giant drill between my knees.

The easiest way to measure the thickness of ice over water is to make a hole, and that's exactly what I was doing. My gloved hands gripped the industrial drill unit, which was attached to three interlocked meter-long screw bits connected end to end, but I still hadn't penetrated to water.

"I think we need another flight," I said. "This ice is more than three meters thick."

About a dozen people gathered around me on the ice surface, wearing identical Big Red parkas with name tags, watching with appreciation. We were all learning the basics of sea ice safety in a survival-oriented course. For an entire day, an instructor named Matt coached us on the intricacies of traveling and operating machinery on the frozen surface of the Ross Sea. Mostly, as it turned out, this involved a lot of drilling to determine ice thickness in different spots.

The entire three-meter bit was immersed in ice. I eased off the power trigger and slowly reversed the drill out of its hole. Soon, as I lifted glove over glove, the drill itself swayed high above my head while I grasped the long metal bit.

The tip of the apparatus finally popped out of the hole, and John, a greasy mechanic with graying hair and drooping sunglasses, handed me another length of screw to attach. After I snapped it on, the drill bit was four meters long—the length of an upended Mini Cooper.

Back it went into the ice. When the first three meters had been swallowed, the bit hit bottom, and I gunned the drill trigger to keep digging. This was by far the biggest drill I'd ever used, and the job needed every inch. No matter what they say, size does matter.

The interlocking bits were shaped like the shaft of a giant screw a couple inches thick, and ice chips were gradually carried to the surface as the drill sank deeper. A mound of shaved ice piled up around the hole.

"Anyone got some syrup?" I asked. "We could make snow cones."

To gain depth, I worked the machine up and down, like cleaning a stovepipe.

"Pretty thick here," said a woman named Debbie. "But we should hit water soon." She had traveled to McMurdo Station to help with a research project on Mount Erebus, something to do with fumaroles and volcanic science. Her parka seemed to be draped around a solid frame, and tufts of iron-gray hair peeked from under the hood and sunglasses.

It was weird to think that somewhere, a few feet underfoot, an ocean existed. If not for the ice, I could have swum from here directly to the North Pole without hitting land.

The ice drill sank deeper.

Finally, when the fourth meter had nearly disappeared, I felt a release of pressure. The bit spun without resistance. A gush of icy water suddenly spurted from the hole, pooling at my feet.

"Eureka!" I shouted. "This one's a gusher!"

"Good thing it's seawater and not oil," Matt said. "We'd have an environmental cleanup."

We lowered a weighted hook on a string that could grab the underside of the ice, giving an exact measurement of thickness.

"Nice work," Matt said, reading the gauge. "With just under four meters of solid ice, all kinds of machinery are allowed here. You could land a jet if you wanted to."

I handed the drill to several other students, who began dismantling the bit segments and packing pieces into cases.

We looked to Matt for further instruction. "Let's go practice drilling a crack," he said, straight faced.

47

I snickered, but was interrupted by a sudden, urgent question from John. "Hey, who's that?" He pointed a grease-blackened finger across the ice plain into silence.

Way out on the horizon, a solitary dark figure was barely visible silhouetted against the white sea.

"Looks like someone's wandering around on the ice," Debbie said. Her forehead wrinkled and her jacket poofed out. "Who would be out here all alone?"

Matt also looked confused. "I dunno," he said, then repeated, "I really don't know who that is."

On the frozen sea surface, twenty miles from McMurdo, we weren't expecting company.

Excited gesticulations and directions followed within the group as everyone focused on the distant character. Lacking visual references, it was hard to describe where to look.

"OK, position yourself the way my arm is pointing," I said, imitating a signpost, trying to give directions. "Out there on the ice, about a mile away, give or take five miles, uh, straight below the horizon."

"Real specific," grunted a middle-aged woman with massive fluffy earmuffs. I'm not sure how she heard my directions with those things wrapped around her skull, and it took a while to get her pointed in the right direction. But how are you supposed to define a location with no landmarks?

Eventually, everyone among the dozen students spotted the silhouetted form in the distance. It was the only dark speck in an entirely white landscape. All activity ceased as we stood in a line, gazing into the distance.

John, who had been packing the ice drill, set the equipment down while we took an impromptu rest break. The gleaming metal drill bit lay like a fallen barbershop pole on the ice.

We continued watching the mysterious character. Who could it be?

At least it was moving. And it seemed like it was getting closer. The figure was gradually becoming larger and more defined.

"Looks like we might have company in a few minutes," Matt said.

Was it a lost adventurer? Someone from McMurdo Station, flouting the off-base zoning rules? None of us could tell. I felt like a cowboy watching a faraway dust puff.

Size and distance were deceptive on the smooth ice plain. A dark speck could have been a Hershey's wrapper sitting a hundred yards away or a diver's hut two miles away. You couldn't tell the difference without closer investigation. Space took on weird proportions when unconfined.

The speck, though, was definitely approaching. As it materialized, we began to make out a peculiar gait. The figure walked upright, but it waddled from side to side like a duck.

48

Wait a minute.

"Maybe it's not a person," I suggested.

"Unless they're injured," said Debbie.

"Not even an injured person could walk like that," countered John. "I think it's an animal."

"It seems to be interested in us," Matt said. "Look how it's making a beeline right toward us."

"Well, we're the only thing out here," I said. "Wish I had my binoculars."

As the words left my lips, I caught a glint of sunshine, and, in an instant, the form resolved into a distinct pattern of shapes and colors. It appeared to be someone in a tuxedo.

With flippers.

And a beak.

9. Visitor

❋❋❋

"It's a PENGUIN!" I shouted. "An Adélie Penguin! Penguinpenguinpenguin!"

Totally blown away, I jumped up and down. Though penguins are known to wander the area offshore from McMurdo Station, people see them here infrequently.

The rest of the ice-safety class was just as excited, and the group broke into a yammer of chattering and murmuring.

"What? A penguin?"

"No way!"

"What's it doing out here?"

"Maybe it's lost …"

"Or it knows something we don't."

"Awesome!"

Soon, it became clear the penguin was going to join our group. When it was close, the bird broke into a run, moving as fast as its short legs could waddle. It seemed to be just as excited to see us.

This made Matt, our instructor, a bit nervous. "Guys, there are rules about getting close to penguins," he lectured. "You're not supposed to approach them without specific permits. But it's too late for us to run away. Let's just sit quietly on the ice until it moves on."

We all settled down to wait.

The penguin had no such qualms about personal space. It didn't stop running until it had approached within five yards of us. Then the bird finally hesitated, taking slow, measured, questioning, wobbly steps forward.

The penguin stood in wonderment of us, and we sat in complete awe of it. For most of the group, this was the first penguin they'd ever seen. For some, it would also be their last.

I'd only ever seen wild penguins on the Galápagos Islands, and those didn't quite compare with this one. I'd once snorkeled with Galápagos Penguins on a semester abroad while flamingos flew overhead, tropical fish darted past my mask, and bikini-clad tourists jammed the decks of nearby sailboats under the hot equatorial sun. This Adélie Penguin, standing alone on a frozen ocean in Antarctica, seemed to fit the stereotype better, making it much more satisfying.

The bird was supremely curious. It teetered, wobbled, and edged closer, then walked a slow, deliberate circle around us, inspecting the members of our sea ice safety class from every angle.

Then the penguin wandered up to the ice drill, which was still lying flat on the ice where John had left it. Evidently, the drill held extraordinary magnetism. The penguin spent several minutes peering wide eyed at the machinery.

With impeccable manners, the penguin did not touch anything. It carried the air of a gentleman adventurer, eager and friendly, generally reserved, and a bit reckless.

This penguin was healthy and full of energy. Where it had come from, and what it was doing alone in a desolate area of ice, was anyone's guess.

It made two more complete circuits of our group, pausing to assess various views. Then, amazingly, it settled down a few inches from the ice drill, stretched out on its belly, and took a nap.

51

I sat just a few feet from the sleeping penguin. Such trust was incredible in a wild bird. Only in one other place had I seen this behavior in seabirds: the Galápagos Islands. There, as in Antarctica, wildlife evolved without human predators and lacks the fear of people. The Galápagos had more in common with Antarctica than I had imagined.

Our group sat on the ice, snapped photos, and chatted while the penguin slept among us. Maybe it was just looking for a little company.

"Do you think it's lonely?" someone asked.

It was impossible not to anthropomorphize the penguin. The way it walked, moved, and changed expression was incredibly animated for a bird. It was easy to think of it as a very small person, and I felt no shame in making the human comparisons. Even a scientist can appreciate events on an emotional level.

"Maybe it's lost," one person said.

I realized people were looking at me expectantly. Though this was the first penguin I'd seen in Antarctica, I'd already developed a reputation as Bird Man around McMurdo Station, and I guess they figured I should know something about penguins.

"It's probably just exploring," I said. "Penguins can walk incredible distances without using up much energy. Though we're far from open water here, maybe it's hoping to find something exciting on its journey."

"But we're in the middle of nowhere!" exclaimed John. "Why would a penguin want to explore here?"

"Look at yourself," I replied. "You're a bit far from home. How did you end up here?" It was a little deeper than I intended to go, but the question lingered in the chilly air.

"Guess you're right," said John. "None of us should be out here. This isn't how humans are supposed to survive."

"Actually," I said, "we're exactly where we should be. We're explorers."

"All right, guys," Matt said. "Class is back in session. I think the penguin is waking up."

Sure enough, the bird had finished its power nap. It used its flippers to push itself back to its feet. Then it waddled a few inches toward us, blinked a few times, turned around, and started ambling away.

We watched it go. The penguin walked unhurriedly, but steadily covered distance until it was once again a speck on the white plain. It had apparently grown bored with our company.

I was surprised how quickly the horizon swallowed it up.

This individual penguin was special enough, but it was all alone, like one person standing inside an empty stadium or a candle in a dark theater. It disappeared in this landscape like a breath of air in outer space.

Circumstances were about to change. Within a week, I'd be surrounded by three hundred thousand penguins.

10. Home

❆❆❆

It's an inevitable question.

"What got you into birding?"

To reply, I sit back, smile, and ask the asker: "What got you so interested in eating, sleeping, walking, and talking?"

Truth is, I don't remember exactly where the obsession started. Birds are like trees, clouds, and Mexican restaurants—generally widespread. Practically everyone in the world sees birds every day. It's just a matter of paying attention.

Curious people often follow up with other predictable questions, so I tend to elaborate: "My favorite bird is the Turkey Vulture because it would eat your dead body. The rarest bird I've seen is a Little Bunting, which I'm pretty sure you've never heard of. I've vomited on half the world's continents looking for birds so far. My biggest pet peeve is being asked about my biggest pet peeves."

And, yes, I'm a natural blond.

Few twenty-two-year-old males equate tits and boobies with the families Paridae and Sulidae, or obsess about primary projection of Empidonax flycatchers. My peers don't generally devour field guides like mystery novels, and not many starving students would unload $1,000 on a pair of specialized image-stabilization binoculars.

So what? I admit it. Birds are my drug. I get high when they fly. Apocalyptic things would happen if I stopped watching birds. I'm an addict. Get over it.

But, why birds?

Unlike most young bird junkies (a thin group), I didn't catch the first impulse from my parents. Neither one—statistician nor newspaper reporter—could tell a swallow from a woodcock. I was neither indoctrinated nor gently introduced to birds within the family. When I started sneaking around woodlots, my mom and dad raised eyebrows, but encouraged my pursuit above other adolescent vices.

Likewise, my school friends weren't remotely interested in birding. I tended to hang in athletic circles surrounding my other obsession, competitive tennis. The sports jocks had no idea I was spending hours after tennis matches identifying ducks at the local sewage ponds, raptor gazing at the airport, and stalking sparrows at the landfill, occasionally hustled by security in all three places. Tennis and birding weren't mutually exclusive; they were just separate activities. While not quite living a double life, I generally kept the nerdy bits to myself.

In retrospect, I really never stood a chance. I've been obsessed by birds as long as I can remember. Whether nurture or nature, my habit was practically set from birth.

When I turned one month old, my parents transplanted to the country on an inheritance from my grandma, who died three days before I was born. They paid cash on a twenty-acre homestead outside Eugene, Oregon, complete with its original one-hundred-year-old home. The house creaked in a thousand different places, but, at the end of a dead-end road, surrounded by idyllic forest, it offered a perfectly peaceful and quiet place to start a family.

At least, that was the theory. Our new house was peaceful enough. But anyone who has lived in the forest knows it's definitely not quiet. We moved there in early spring, when people sleep with windows open to warm breezes and songbirds are jacked up on hormones. The country birds chattered and hooted louder than city traffic.

My parents still grumble about it: "Why does it have to be so loud around here? Those stupid birds woke us up at four in the morning!"

Dawn chorus is indeed deafening, especially in spring. Robins, grosbeaks, warblers, and dozens of other species sing most energetically as the sun rises, proclaiming their territories with a variety of whistles, warbles, and screeches. Collectively, they're louder than an alarm clock.

My mom and dad complain most about a particularly loud and repetitive dawn choruser—the Olive-sided Flycatcher. From April to August, starting at 4:30 a.m. and continuing through late morning, this bird declares its territory in our yard with a unique three-part whistle, repeated once every fifteen to twenty seconds from the tip of a dead cherry tree. Like an annoying jingle, this tune is best described with a lyrical mnemonic:

"Quick, THREE beers!"

As a contented infant, I slept though it all. In early formative years, my brain probably processed these bird sounds alongside words and physical noises. Some parents play Bach music or foreign-language tapes to their babies, hoping for positive effects on intelligence. I think bird song entered my consciousness at a very early age, for good or ill.

When I took my first breath, my mom breathed a sigh of relief. She promised, "Never again!" after nine months of vomiting ranked hers in the 99th percentile of most miserable pregnancies. The upshot was that I never received siblings. Considering stereotypes, I take it as a compliment when people are surprised to learn I'm an only child, but relish the extra freedom associated with such status. I've never needed to scrap for day-to-day existence, so I can pick my battles wisely.

56   My first memories are snapshot outdoor images, mostly involving animals: a cat stuck up a tree, chickens in our chicken coop, a Great Horned Owl swooping out of a willow. When I was about two, my dad once found me sitting cross-legged around a pile of deer poo, popping the pellets like chocolate M&Ms. (I'd always thought this was weird until I recently watched survivalist Bear Grylls do exactly the same thing on *Man vs. Wild*, the Discovery Channel TV show. Apparently deer poo has caloric value because the animals' digestion works too fast to fully absorb nutrients. Rabbits eat their own turds at least one more time for the same reason. Who knew?)

Over the first few years, I spent a lot of time outdoors, often alone, exploring my twenty-acre backyard, bordered by Bureau of Land Management and Weyerhaeuser Co. forests. Though I was somewhat isolated, I can't think of a better way to grow up. I was typically muddy, scratched up, and grass stained, chasing snakes and building dams, feasting on wild huckleberries and climbing trees.

I didn't worry about naming things. There were yellow birds and red ones, and I knew their differences by experience. Classification would come later.

When people now see young pictures of me, their reaction is always the same: "What happened? You used to be so cute!"

Mini-me had nearly white hair, freckles, Harry Potter glasses, and a very large hat size, and ranked second-shortest in his class: I was a joker, inquisitive, and always active.

At age five, I started playing piano. At eight, I picked up a tennis racket for the first time. But I don't know exactly when I flipped my first field guide or focused my first pair of binoculars. Birding, for me, was a gradual, insidious, and unforeseen addiction.

Around fifth grade, though, things suddenly got serious. I transferred to a small private school called Oak Hill nestled among a tract of prime oak savanna on the edge of town. Each classroom possessed a single large window overlooking the forest. My sly fifth-grade teacher, recognizing an opportunity, installed a clear plastic bird feeder with suction cups on our window. When a new bird showed up, she interrupted class to consult field guides and backyard bird posters.

In retrospect, that fifth-grade bird feeder changed my life. I realized that birds followed neat patterns. The yellow ones were American Goldfinches and the red ones Purple Finches. To a packrat kid who hoarded everything from used postage stamps to business cards and toilet paper rolls, this was immensely satisfying. Identifying a bird for the first time was like adding it to the collection.

Somehow, alone in my class, I caught the birding bug. How or why I can't tell, but a seed had taken root.

57

11. Crozier

✳✳✳

In 1841, Sir James Clark Ross sailed into new territory—and history books—when his two wooden ships, HMS *Erebus* and HMS *Terror*, entered an unknown Antarctic sea. Ross' expedition reached farther south than anyone had previously ventured, and this record would stand another fifty-eight years before competing teams raced for the South Pole. On his return, Ross was knighted, nominated to the Legion d'Honneur, and eventually died of heavy drinking in Aylesbury, England.

Today, his name is plastered everywhere down south.

That cold sea, south of New Zealand, is now called the Ross Sea. Its frigid waters bite a chunk from Antarctica's pancake-like contour, extending farther south than any other ocean. The Ross Sea is a bleak place, except underwater. Incredibly rich concentrations of phytoplankton support dense marine life, from microscopic bacteria to whales. In 2007, long-line fishermen here accidentally snagged a Colossal Squid thirty-three feet long and weighing more than one thousand pounds—the largest squid ever documented.

A cluster of mountains emerges from the west edge of the sea, forming Ross Island. The island is often mistaken for part of the Antarctic mainland, since the intervening ocean lies buried under a thick, floating ice sheet the size of France. This blanket, called the Ross Ice Shelf, collects the runoff of several large glaciers.

Ross Island, just shy of one hundred miles across, contains two gnarly volcanoes, each named somewhat darkly for one of Ross' ships: Mount Erebus and Mount Terror. Erebus is the taller twin, reaching well over twelve thousand feet, qualifying the island as Earth's sixth highest. Erebus is also the world's southernmost active volcano and usually issues a wispy plume from its icy summit. Residents are relaxed about the mountain's activity.

Crozier

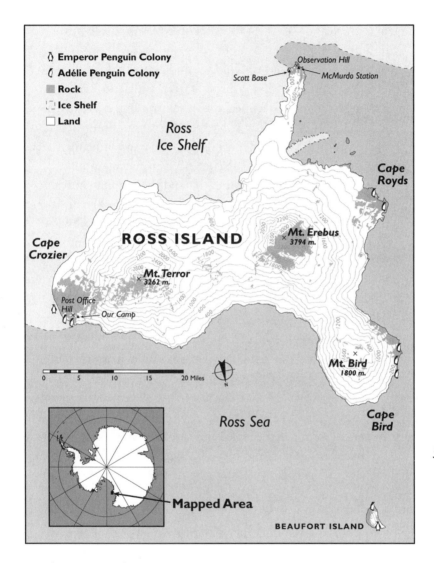

Map by Grace Gardner

When the volcano is talking to us, people reason, it's happy. When it goes all quiet, watch out.

Today, the island houses twin U.S. and New Zealand settlements, respectively McMurdo Station and Scott Base. The environmental group Greenpeace also set up camp on Ross Island in the late 1980s to encourage Antarctic Treaty nations to declare the entire continent a World Park. After five years of being politely ignored, Greenpeace discontinued the occupation.

Several penguin colonies scatter around the island's shores. The largest sits at Cape Crozier, in the lee of Mount Terror at the island's eastern tip. Crozier carries the name of Francis Crozier, captain of the HMS *Terror*, and, more pertinently, Sir James Clark Ross' best friend.

Once Cape Crozier was on the map, other explorers followed—slowly. In 1902, the British Discovery Expedition, including luminary Antarctic explorers Robert Scott and Ernest Shackleton, became the first to land at Crozier. They erected a giant wooden post on a rocky ridgetop, visible from sea, to serve as a pre-arranged message point. Mail could be left there for later parties. More than one hundred years later, that weathered wooden post still stands at Crozier, reminding penguin researchers of a time before GPS and satellite Internet.

60 The Discovery Expedition further scouted and charted Crozier, making several visits to the eastern tip of Ross Island. A scouting party led by Charles Royds discovered the small Emperor Penguin colony there later in 1902. On one aborted attempt to reach Crozier from the other side of Ross Island, a group of explorers became trapped in a blizzard, and, in trying to navigate among broken ice, one man slid over a cliff. His body was never recovered.

Priorities on the Discovery Expedition soon turned to marching south. Shackleton collapsed with scurvy, Scott called him a wuss, and, after two years of reconnoitering the area, the expedition returned to England. Shackleton would command his own heroic Antarctic journey ten years later, solidifying a longstanding place among legendary explorers. Meanwhile, penguins continued to inhabit Cape Crozier, no doubt amused by their occasional human visitors.

Robert Scott, marching toward destiny, returned to lead the British Antarctic Expedition in 1910, goaded more by glory (and his wife) than anything else. This time, he aimed for South Pole fame, racing against Roald Amundsen's Norwegian team to reach the end of the Earth. Scott made some mistakes—for instance, he relied on ill-adapted horses to haul equipment across the ice—and, after a marathon march, famously tagged the pole thirty-four days after Amundsen had done so. Slowed by a poor diet and shamed by their second-place finish, Scott's party starved to death on the return trip eleven miles from a depot of food after having marched more than seventeen hundred miles across barren ice. Their journals, and corpses, were recovered by a search party months later.

Before this disaster, though, Cape Crozier's penguins received some new visitors. Scott's expedition had overwintered on Ross Island, poised for their ill-fated journey while awaiting daylight and warmer temperatures. In mid-winter, the restless explorers wallowed in boredom. Three men decided to take a side trip to Cape Crozier in hopes of collecting Emperor Penguin eggs.

Emperor Penguins, they thought, ranked among the most primitive species on Earth. So they figured an Emperor's embryo might reveal some insights about evolution. If the penguins were crazy enough to lay eggs in mid-winter, indicated by Royds' discovery of chicks in early summer, so be it. The small party set off for the long, dark march to Cape Crozier.

The winter journey was more severe than they had reckoned. In perpetual darkness, the marchers lost the route, hauling sledges through mile after mile of heavily crevassed ice. Often, when a man dropped into a hidden crevasse, only thin sled traces held him dangling over abyssal death. Temperatures dropped to nearly eighty degrees below zero. Their sleeping bags and clothing froze into solid sheets of armor. In one blizzard, the three men spent several days lying in an igloo, a scant few miles from Crozier. When the roof of their igloo blew off, they thought the game was up, and penned goodbye letters to distant loved ones.

Incredibly, though, the blizzard abated, and the party of penguin seekers persevered to reach Cape Crozier. They found the Emperor Penguins incubating eggs—never before observed by human eyes—and collected several embryos, carting them carefully back to Scott's base camp. The entire one-hundred-fifty-mile trip took more than a month. Ultimately, the penguin eggs weren't very useful to science, and nothing much good came of the excursion until Apsley Cherry-Garrard, youngest of the three Crozier explorers, later recounted his experiences of the trip in a book, *The Worst Journey in the World* (1922). This book has been repeatedly named among the best adventure and travel stories of all time.

Cherry-Garrard was twenty-four when he walked to Cape Crozier. Almost exactly one hundred years later, I would belt in to a helicopter to follow his tracks. At twenty-two, I felt eerily reincarnated, another kid excited about penguins and expectant of imminent adventure. I felt close to Cherry. What's a hundred years of ice and snow, mostly untouched by humans? History could have happened yesterday.

62   Sadly, Cherry-Garrard never again did anything so exciting. After returning to England, he became disillusioned, battled clinical depression, married late in life, and died of what was only described as "illness" at age seventy-three. The wide-eyed, daring Antarctic adventure marked a singular moment in the otherwise bland rich kid's life.

But these events were far from my mind as I eagerly anticipated my first visit to Cape Crozier.

12. Snowcraft

✳✳✳

It was ten below zero when I dug my coffin.

I stood on an endless surface of level snow with no shelter in sight. On one horizon, Mount Erebus rose starkly white against the blue sky, a wisp of smoke wafting from its volcanic summit. In the other direction, distant peaks of the Antarctic mainland formed a long, sawtoothed line. As long as clouds didn't blot out this view, the weather would stay calm for at least a few hours, since the worst blizzards generally blew in from the south.

Physical work was the best way to stay warm. On the flat, featureless plain, survival started with body heat. To set up my coffin, I outlined a rectangle four feet wide by eight feet long on the snow's surface and began digging. First, I incised the perimeter of the rectangle with a snow saw, a thin metal blade with one serrated edge that could sink vertically into layers of packed snow. I worked around my line, slicing a thin groove several feet deep. Then I used a square-bladed shovel to start excavating the pit inside the cuts.

63

Sweat dripped off my nose, freezing wherever it landed. I soon stripped to thermal shirtsleeves, hoping to avoid sweating too much. When I stopped working, the perspiration would solidify in my clothing, turning the fabric to cardboard.

In about two hours, the trench was four feet deep. I knelt down, trying to assess whether the floor was flat. In a dress rehearsal, I tossed the shovel aside, climbed down into the snow coffin, lay flat in its chilly depths, and stretched out on my back. Arms crossed over my chest, eyes to the skies, I reclined in my icy grave like a corpse.

Someone whistled. "Looks comfy—how's the fit?"

Nick, the instructor of my Snowcraft I outdoor survival class, stood on the lip of my tomb, staring down.

I flopped around a bit and showers of dry snow crystals cascaded onto my face. Knobs of hard ice stabbed into my back. This coffin wasn't the least bit comfortable. "It's great!" I lied. "I'll sleep like a baby."

Nick narrowed his eyes but didn't argue. With a gloved hand, he swept an unruly strand of hair from his sunglasses and said, stepping back from the edge: "Nice work. Just make sure your sleeping pad will fit in there. It makes all the difference. And mark your trench with a black flag so nobody falls in it."

Another pair of feet appeared against the sky, knocking more snow into my hole. "Watch it!" I warned. "I don't really feel like being buried alive in here." I sat up, brushing off loose snow like dandruff. The top of my head was still below ground level when I sat straight.

Jeremy, a janitor from the Midwest, peered down. From my angle, his jutting chin and Big Red were silhouetted against a patch of brilliantly blue sky. "Man, how did you dig that so fast? My trench is, like, half the depth."

In reply, I imitated an evil laugh, slowly rose out of my grave, and dramatically intoned: "I am the undead ..."

Jeremy fled in mock fright to his own excavation site a dozen yards away, yelling something about square-bladed versus rounded shovels.

Snowcraft I, or Snow School, is the flagship course of the Field Services Training Program (F-Stop) at McMurdo Station. Everyone calls the class "Happy Campers," and it's a rite of passage for many Antarctic recruits. Anybody headed for a deep field camp must attend this intensive survival training before cutting loose from civilization. In the class, search-and-rescue specialists teach skills related to camping in Antarctica, like how to light a liquid-fuel camp stove, operate a VHF radio, and clip on a helicopter seat harness.

The real initiation, though, comes when Happy Campers are trucked out, dumped, and left alone on a barren spot on the ice plain, as if they'd been stranded in a helicopter crash and had to wait for help to arrive. Students work together, using the skills

64

they've learned, to set up a temporary camp, dig in, and spend the coldest hours outdoors, while their instructors sleep in a warm hut nearby.

My Snow School class was ready for the challenge.

After Ivan the Terrabus rumbled us to a remote spot outside McMurdo Station, about thirty of us stood grouped on the ice, watching Ivan recede into the distance. A pile of survival gear remained with us.

Our instructor, Nick, got right to business: "As you can see, we're stuck here on a flat, snowy wilderness. There's no shelter in sight."

Like jailbirds plotting their escape, everyone turned to stare at the green, warm, cozy buildings of Scott Base, the New Zealand Antarctic station, hazily visible a mile or two in the distance, with its carpeted, single-room bar, decorated with stuffed Kiwis and artistic photography. But Nick was one step ahead: "Anyone who sneaks over to Scott Base for a beer will regret it. As far as you're concerned, we've survived a helicopter crash thousands of miles from civilization. And help won't arrive until tomorrow."

A well-built woman with gray hair and eyeglasses raised her hand, interrupting to complain: "I'm cold!"

We'd been outdoors for twenty minutes, and already several Happy Campers were unhappy, edging toward discomfort, visibly shifting from one foot to another, gloved hands stuffed deep in pockets, with clenched and determined expressions. I didn't blame them. It was ten below, and a wicked breeze blew across the plain. The wind chill must have been frigid.

"All right," Nick said. "Everyone spread out. We're gonna do some jumping jacks. If you get cold out here, start moving. Ready? One, two, three, four ..."

Thirty identically dressed Happy Campers lined up on the frozen Antarctic plain, formed ranks like the Dallas Cheerleaders, and pounded out an endless set of jumping jacks.

When we gasped icy air into our lungs, Nick relented. "OK, now turn to the person next to you and inspect their face. Look

65

for little white spots on the nose and cheeks, which would signify frostnip, an early stage of frostbite."

The guy next to me was a middle-aged professor with a neatly trimmed beard. We confronted each other's faces. Other than some loose strands of coyote fur shaken from the hood lining of our Big Reds, we appeared clean.

Over the rest of the afternoon, Nick encouraged, prodded, and cajoled us into constructing a weatherproof snow camp, stopping every now and then to exercise and check for frostnip. First, we set up three sturdy Scott tents in a line perpendicular to the prevailing wind. The central tent became the cooking tent, equipped with a stove ready to melt snow and boil water. We quarried and stacked snow blocks in the spaces between these tents to form a wind barrier. In the lee of this wall, we erected two mountain tents—typical of backpacking expeditions in warmer climates—and, downwind of the mountain tents, stacked any heavy objects that could dislodge in a gale. Equipment like snowmobiles or metal shovels could break loose in a storm and blow right through a tent, so it's best to store it downwind.

Then we made a Quincy hut by piling suitcases, backpacks, and other bulky items in a heap and covering them with two or three feet of shoveled snow. After packing the snow down, we dug a tunnel below ground level that emerged underneath the mound. We evacuated the suitcases through the tunnel, leaving a sizeable hollow, like a frozen beaver lodge, big enough to sleep three or four people. The Quincy resembled an igloo with an underground entrance except it was made with snow instead of ice blocks.

Finally, when our base looked like a refugee camp on Mount Everest, Nick gathered his troops to offer one last option for shelter: "What if you were all alone, stuck in the cold without a tent, and had to survive for twenty-four hours?"

Not a thrilling prospect.

"Assuming you had a shovel, you could dig yourself a snow coffin. It might help you survive the night. And, if you died in it, at least you'd be buried properly."

No one laughed.

"The idea is simple. Just dig a grave-shaped hole in the snow, big enough to lie inside but small enough to trap body heat, and cover it with a sled or snow blocks. It's the closest thing to instant shelter out here. Who's interested?"

Out of thirty students, only four of us elected to dig our own trenches. I loved the idea. How many people have ever slept inside an Antarctic glacier?

And so it was that, two hours later, I carved the finishing touches on a first-class ice coffin. My pit was deep and wide enough to lie flat inside, and roofed with several large rectangular snow blocks. Steps led underground from one end. Down this hole went my sleeping pad and heavy-duty sleeping bag. Above ground, I planted a black flag on a bamboo pole.

As evening approached, sunshine slanted from a low angle. Shadows of inland volcanoes drew long patterns on the ice. The temperature dropped with indirect exposure to the sun. When a stray cloud blocked the sun entirely, cold tentacles slithered through every gap in my clothing.

My waiting coffin was looking less inviting at fifteen below.

"Hey, man, your edifice looks like an Egyptian tomb," said Jeremy the janitor. He stood next to me, regarding the entrance. A geometric staircase descended into darkness, framed by massive rectangular snow blocks.

"Better not trespass," I warned. "I booby-trapped it. And I have an army of zombies ready to defend this tomb."

Jeremy smirked. "Yah, and I've got the perfect offensive weapon—a square-bladed shovel!"

"Shovels can't defeat zombies," I argued. "Zombies are already dead, remember."

Jeremy had been an alternate janitor for the McMurdo season. When another janitor suddenly dropped out, Jeremy was in, with less than two weeks to get ready. He complained about last-minute physicals, plane tickets, and paperwork, but relished his one chance to have an Antarctic adventure. Every job at McMurdo Station is competitive.

I sauntered over to the pee flag a hundred yards outside camp. In Antarctica, a yellow flag on a bamboo pole means only one thing: Urinate Here. Guys have it easy. Over time, the fluttering yellow flag accumulated a frozen yellow mound of ice. The sight of so much frozen pee was oddly fascinating, but my tomb awaited.

Relinquishing my idea to stay up all night, and thus thwart the necessity of sleeping in the snow, I wormed headfirst into my coffin. Inside, a bluish light penetrated the darkness. The bulky Big Red, wind pants, boots, gloves, and hat impeded navigation in the confined space. I reached up and slid a snow block over the entrance, sealing myself underground.

Without removing a single item of clothing, I slithered inside my sleeping bag. My alarm clock's battery had frozen. The battery of my camera, tucked inside my sleeping bag, would freeze, too, before morning, as would a canteen of water snuggled next to my feet.

Thus entombed, with half my belongings stuffed in my sleeping bag, I regarded the layer of ice barricading me from the world. Every little rustle brought fistfuls of loose snow onto my face. The grave was eerily quiet in its depths, like a crevasse.

My bed was actually pretty comfortable, as long as I didn't move around too much. I downed a chocolate bar and rested flat on my back, thinking murkily about Condition One blizzards, penguins, and zombies.

Not even the Abominable Snowman could stop me from sleeping like a baby.

13. Bucketheads

✳✳✳

The next morning found me ready for action with a sense of humor, a rope in one hand, and a white plastic bucket inverted over my head.

We Happy Campers looked ridiculous. After retreating indoors to warm up after our night out (nobody in this group had contracted frostbite, unlike earlier cohorts, and the weather had held steady, unlike in previous weeks), we launched immediately into the next phase of survival training.

To simulate whiteout conditions, we wore white buckets over our heads, incidentally the same kind I'd soon be using in lieu of a loo. With every movement, my bucket clanged into walls, standing objects, or other people's buckets, leaving my brain ringing. If this was like a whiteout, I sure hoped I'd never have to rescue anybody.

Today, though, that's exactly what we were supposed to do. We were told that a man had exited the building during a storm and become lost in the whiteout. Somewhere within a hundred yards of the door, an instructor sat outside on bare snow. We were tasked with venturing outdoors, finding the "lost victim," and guiding him back in. Super easy—without the buckets. Our bucket-blinded class hatched a simple plan. We'd hold on to a hundred-yard rope at equal intervals, deploy ourselves to full stretch, then do two semicircular sweeps and hope someone tripped over the target before following the rope to safety. The plan turned out to be a recipe for chaos.

Just try sometime to walk with your eyes closed. You don't walk straight. In 2003, a high school student named Andrea Axtell illustrated this with a simple experiment in which she blindfolded test subjects and had them start walking from one end of a football field to the other. Of several dozen volunteers, none made it to the opposite goal line before veering to one of the sidelines, and the paths they followed were directly related to handedness (right-handed people curved left and left-handed people curved right) and height (shorter people walked in tighter arcs). In other words, without visual cues, people literally walk in circles.

On the ice, with buckets over our heads, we Happy Campers were doomed from the start. We happily clanked out the door in an orderly line, linked by the rope, thinking this was going to be a cinch. What could be easier than finding someone less than a hundred yards away who wasn't even trying to hide?

When my turn came, I was yanked outside by a sudden pull on the rope. I tried to follow the same direction as the guy six feet in front of me, but the plan quickly deteriorated. Soon, it was so difficult to stay afoot on the ice that all thoughts of direction were scrapped in favor of just hanging on to the rope.

I covered a few dozen yards in this way, bumping and slipping in my own world of white. It became easier to half squat as I moved along, feeling ahead as much as possible and keeping a broadly planted base between my feet.

The guy in front of me tripped and fell, smashing his bucketed face to the ground. He grimly held on to the rope for a while, trying to regain his footing while being dragged along. He lost track of the rope and frantically groped for it until I came up behind, equally blind but still walking with the rope. Without warning, I stumbled into his body and we both went down hard, buckets clanking.

"Do you have the rope?" I shouted.

My voice reverberated inside the white plastic bucket, making my head spin.

He shouted something back, which to me sounded like, "Eh willat borderpolt cole!"

"I can't hear you. Do you have the rope?" I yelled.

He made some reply, but it was no use. We made no progress yelling into our own ears. We just crouched on the ice, inches apart, yelling and gesticulating at each other with white plastic buckets over our heads, each unable to understand the other.

Although I still gripped the rope, it had stopped moving. Up and down the line, people were encountering similar difficulties. I could hear muffled shouts from behind me, but had no idea what was going on. The class had pre-arranged a signal of three sharp tugs to communicate when the rope was deployed to its full length, but now the line was being jerked forward and back in random bursts.

I sat on the ice and tried to figure out how to proceed. Without being able to coordinate with the other Happy Campers strung out on the ice, we couldn't make an orderly rescue search. I could try to be a hero, leave the rope, and wander blindly in hopes of locating the victim myself, but then it would be impossible to navigate back to safety, even if by a miracle I found him. For once, I understood the desperate nature of rescue missions. Even a highly trained crew would have a hard time with this operation.

After a minute, I felt a tap on my shoulder. Someone gently lifted the weight off my head. Suddenly, I was blinking in the bright sunshine of midday, eyes adjusting to sparkling white in every direction, feeling foolish.

Nick, my instructor, grinned as he twirled my bucket. "Bang, you're dead," he said. "Frozen and lost in a blizzard, along with the victim and your entire search party."

I tried to think of a more fitting sound effect for freezing to death.

Nick continued, "International media already picked up the story. Headlines say, 'Tragedy in Antarctica: Americans Mismanage Rescue Operation.' Hope your family didn't love you too much."

I thought of home, thousands of miles away, and resolved to email a real update that very evening. It was hard to stay in touch, but, as this exercise so pointedly demonstrated, life was on the line out here every single day.

Happy Campers straggled back toward the classroom, dangling buckets. One guy commented, "Bevis and Buckethead, huh? Well, we all kicked the bucket, anyway. Check this one off the bucket list!"

"You were all pretty entertaining, I admit," Nick said. "Like a herd of blind penguins. Don't worry. Only a third of survival classes locate their victim in this exercise. It's pretty tough. We mostly do it to demonstrate how difficult rescue operations can be."

"Glad it wasn't for real," Jeremy the janitor piped up. All around, people looked happy to be alive.

When a real storm arrived, I hoped things would go a bit more smoothly. At least I wouldn't be wearing a bucket over my head.

14. Flying Machines

"If the helicopter crashes," the helitech advised, "lean forward and cup your hands on your knees. That way, when you hit ground, your spine won't snap."

Michelle, Kirsten, and I stood grouped in the tiny McMurdo Station helicopter hangar office, listening to a pre-flight safety talk.

After a stressful week in McMurdo Station, we were ready for an onslaught of penguins. Sling loads had flown ahead of us, so tents and propane tanks were waiting at the Crozier field camp. Everything else, our personal baggage and penguin gear, was piled in a heap on the gravel helipad outside, including enough food to last the three of us for three months. It looked like a lot of stuff. I couldn't help but think about what was being left behind. Showers, beds, crispy iceberg lettuce—the accoutrements of civilization.

"The other guy said to sit straight against the seat," Michelle interrupted. She tucked a wayward strand of blonde hair under her soft hat. "Which is it?"

The helitech paused. "Either way, you're toast. So don't worry too much."

Toast? More like pancaked and popsicled.

The helo office was cold and mostly bare. Against one wall stood a shelf of helicopter helmets. On the facing end, a greasy desk sat wedged alongside a metal baggage scale. The only other amenities were a comfy couch and box of stale snacks. This would be our last glimpse of society for three months.

Outside, another helitech loaded boxes of gear onto a red Bell 212 Twin Huey, parked squarely on its concrete pad outside. The helicopter gleamed in bright, sunny, and clear conditions—perfect for flying.

Weather over the past week had been dicey. While we packed gear in McMurdo Station, eyes to the skies, Antarctic winds seesawed and gusted. Cape Crozier, on the exposed tip of Ross Island, is generally much windier than McMurdo, so anything less than perfect weather was worrisome.

Two days before departure, Kirsten and I watched a helicopter zipping overhead at McMurdo, dangling a sling load, heading toward Crozier. Later, over dinner in the cafeteria, a helitech confirmed that the sling load held our tents and propane tanks, but that the aircraft had encountered high winds and turned around mid-flight. It usually takes fifty-mile-per-hour gusts to dissuade a landing. We hoped for better luck on our own commute to the Crozier field camp.

As it happened, on flight day the weather couldn't have been better.

"Okay, let's go," the helitech said. The pilot, already ensconced in his throne, beckoned to us from within his bug-eyed windshield.

Our penguin crew straggled across the wide gravel helipad, striding toward the gleaming aircraft. A large pile of boxed food waited next to the helicopter's cargo hold, and we formed a supply line to load gear.

I was amped. This was my first-ever trip in a helicopter—and in Antarctica, no less. It wasn't just me. The whole crew bristled with adrenaline. Something about these flying machines sets the heart racing. When rotors start spinning and engines engage, life kicks into overdrive.

Michelle, Kirsten, and I jammed in a narrow slot behind the cockpit, facing backward, against a wall of boxed gear filling the cargo space. We donned helmets and harnesses, plugged into communications headsets, and checked straps.

I wondered if penguins ever wished they could fly.

The pilot skillfully lifted off, rotated, angled forward, and accelerated into the Antarctic sky. McMurdo Station shrank behind as we rapidly chopped above the frozen coastline toward Cape Crozier.

The National Science Foundation maintains a fleet of four helicopters at McMurdo to service outlying field research camps. The aircraft constantly ply the skies, under tight schedules to ferry supplies and personnel around remote parts of Ross Island and vicinity. These red helicopters are a familiar sight overhead, like prehistoric beasts against the timeless environment; they seem to move with the lively grace of a pterodactyl.

Of course, the spirit of the helicopter fleet emanates from the pilots, some of the most skilled and experienced in the world. To fly over The Ice, they have trained for years in other brutal conditions. Many Antarctic helicopter pilots learned their trade in various militaries. During the off season, pilots take seasonal jobs in the Arctic, servicing offshore oil rigs or other remote installations.

Pressing the in-flight intercom, I asked our pilot if he'd ever crashed.

"Back in the army," he replied, in a proper British accent, "I had a buzzard come through the windscreen once. Broken glass and bloody bird parts all over the cockpit. Never fell out of the sky, though, if that's what you mean."

He seemed calm enough. But Ross Island has a long history of aircraft accidents.

Between 1946 and 1966, about twenty-seven enlisted men died in eight separate U.S. Navy airplane and helicopter crashes near McMurdo Station. And in November 1969, a geologist and a New Zealand film director died after their helicopter dropped and slid seven hundred feet near Mount McLennan.

In January 1971, a Coast Guard helicopter crash-landed in a sudden downdraft on the northwest flank of Mount Erebus. The passengers included a writer on his way to visit penguin researchers at Cape Bird on the northern tip of Ross Island. They all survived but were stranded without survival gear for about twelve hours before rescuers arrived. The mostly intact helicopter is still visible on the mountain, now partially drifted with snow.

In November 1979, a commercial jet from New Zealand smashed into a different flank of Mount Erebus, pulverizing all 257 passengers and crew. The disaster marked an abrupt end to a two-year series of sightseeing tours organized by Air New Zealand, designed as day trips with special guides, like Sir Edmund Hillary of Everest mountaineering fame, to point out landmarks through the cabin windows. Hillary had been scheduled to guide the doomed flight but cancelled due to other commitments.

More recently, in October 1992, two civilians perished in a helicopter crash at the Cape Royds penguin colony on Ross Island. And, in January 2003, a pilot and scientist were evacuated with injuries after a sling load bounced into the rotors and their helicopter plummeted at Dry Valleys near McMurdo Station.

As we swept over ice plains and white mountainsides, past disasters never entered my mind. I was too busy taking in the incredible scenery below. We glided along massive ice shelves, crevasse fields, and volcanic cones, frozen in time and space. For one ten-minute period, we followed a giant ice cliff delineating Ross Island's contour. The ice wall towered higher than our flying altitude, close enough to just about reach out and touch it. Discussion among the helicopter's passengers and crew required the intercom, so conversations were brief and sparse. Rhythmic rotor sounds and engine growls added white noise to the white landscape. Each of us watched Ross Island drift by, occupied with silent thoughts.

My own thoughts scattered. Would the penguins be friendly? I wished polar bears lived in Antarctica, but, reconsidering, I didn't wish too hard. How much water would I save by not showering or flushing a toilet for three months? I thought of home. I wondered what Michelle and Kirsten were thinking behind their sunglasses, thick parkas, and impassive expressions. I snapped photos from every conceivable angle.

More than anything, I hoped for a fantastic field season.

The pilot's voice broke my reverie.

"That's Cape Crozier," he announced, as we chopped breathtakingly low over a pass between ridges and mountains—except, like a true Brit, he pronounced it *Crozah*. "Welcome home!"

15. Touchdown

❄❄❄

As our helicopter landed at Cape Crozier, I imagined the arrival here of Apsley Cherry-Garrard one hundred years before. He must have looked upon the same landscape. The view hadn't changed much in the intervening century.

The scene is dominated by a broad U-shaped valley full of ice swept up toward rocky ridgelines on both sides. From the air, several small peaks are visible in the area, protruding through the snow cover like skyscrapers in a fog bank. Rocky hilltops trail slanted lines of boulder fields that hint at erosive forces on a geologic scale. Here is where land meets sea, but it is difficult to discern the difference. Both are covered in a thick armor of ice.

On the downslope horizon, frozen ocean meanders into the distance, flanked by the edge of the Ross Ice Shelf contouring and ending abruptly in a fifty-foot ice cliff. Upslope, ridgelines and glaciers leapfrog all the way to the summit of Mount Terror more than two vertical miles above. This is raw terrain unmarked by human prints. In the frozen space, time slows perceptibly.

I sensed some of the excitement that must have overtaken Cherry's party as they arrived at Crozier. Their arrival mirrored my own. Like me, Cherry came for the penguins, and must have cultivated the same anticipation of approaching the strange birds. I couldn't wait to get near them.

For the first-time traveler, though, Crozier holds its spectacle carefully hidden. The penguin colony lies a mile from camp, and is shielded by a rocky peak and ridgeline. As the helicopter settled, I craned through cargo netting and peered outside.

"Where are the birds?" I asked.

"They don't wander up to camp very often," Kirsten replied. "Usually, you can't see a single penguin from here."

Sure enough, nothing moved outside. You'd have no idea that a quarter-million birds sat right around the corner. I'd have to wait one more day to walk among penguins.

I couldn't stop thinking about Cherry. Like me, he was in his early twenties when he arrived at Crozier, the perfect time to be exploring the end of the Earth. Today, most of my age bracket is transitioning between school and work, paying off student loans, negotiating health insurance, and starting families. As we get older, responsibilities pile up. Never again will we be so free and capable as in young adulthood. Yet most of us push onward, never taking full advantage of the freedom.

As the pilot gently negotiated the landing pad, I glanced over at Kirsten and Michelle, belted securely in their harnesses. Though each had spent previous seasons here, both researchers were fully immersed in the moment.

Of course, a hundred years ago, Cherry had it a bit rougher. His team approached Crozier on foot in midwinter, when darkness blackened the landscape twenty-four hours a day and temperatures dropped to fifty, sixty, even seventy degrees below zero. They were also unlucky to be slammed by a ferocious blizzard in transit, nearly perishing inside an impromptu hut of rock and ice. Today, such a journey, even aided by technological advances of the past century, would still be considered epic (even without the blizzard). The style of Antarctic exploration has changed considerably over the past hundred years while the natural terrain remains constant. In 1910, Cherry couldn't have dreamed of flying around in jets and helicopters. Instead, the entire British Antarctic Expedition sailed from Britain to the frozen continent, then marched overland across the ice, men hauling gear on sleds.

So it was with a sense of privilege and a bit of guilt that I jumped from the shining red Bell 212 to alight on Cape Crozier for the first time. Any thoughts of the past had to be quickly suppressed, however, as we speedily unloaded the helicopter, ducking to avoid its orbiting blades. Landing at Crozier, one of the windiest and most weather-ridden spots on Earth, is always chancy. This time, the pilot stayed in his seat, keeping the engines running and rotors spinning, ready to lift away at any second should the skies close in, while we efficiently transferred equipment.

Within several minutes, we piled enough gear to last three months in a heap at a safe distance. As Kirsten and I ferried the last boxes of frozen food, Michelle fiddled with a handheld VHF radio. "I've established ground communication with the pilot," she yelled over the rotor and engine noise. "We're on our own now!"

Kirsten, Michelle, and I formed a human blanket over the pile of equipment and food in the snow, stretching out face down to weight the lighter boxes against the powerful rotor downdrafts. As the helicopter lifted off, snowy spindrift swirled into a powdery fog around us. For a few seconds, engines screamed in our ears and ice crystallized in our noses. Then the machine was up and away, a red speck growing steadily smaller in a blue sky.

Suddenly, we were alone.

An all-encompassing quiet immediately enveloped us, like the sound-dampened chamber of a woodland snowfall. Even background sounds were muffled. The silence magnified isolation. It took a while to get used to this quiet, though wind would create plenty of white noise on most days.

Was Cherry bothered by stark silences? He probably never had the chance during his time at Crozier, since his party was more concerned with surviving a hurricane-force winter blizzard. Still, isolation probably affected their team. Forced to eat, sleep, and work in close proximity, perhaps they yearned for a little peace once in a while. With separate individual tents, Michelle, Kirsten, and I would command a relatively luxurious field camp.

❋

"The rabbit peeks out of his hole, hops around the tree, and jumps back down its hole. See? Like this."

Hours after landing at Crozier, Kirsten expertly snugged a bowline (pronounced BULL-en) knot in one of my tent's guidelines.

"Rabbit?" I asked. "Tree? We're in Antarctica, remember."

"How about this," I suggested, studying the knot. "The zombie leaps out of his snow cave, lassoes a penguin, and then falls down a crevasse. That seems a little more plausible here."

"Whatever sticks in your memory," Kirsten said. She checked tension on the line, then looked up.

My turn. With thickly gloved hands, tying knots is a little clumsy, but I heeded the warnings from survival school back at McMurdo: Never, ever venture outside to work without gloves. Frostnip lurks in every small task.

Eventually, I threaded the right combination of rabbits, holes, zombies, and crevasses, and we tied the tent ropes to rocks buried in snow. In a landscape without rocks, we would have used a dead man anchor system, knotting ropes to poles slotted perpendicularly in the ice, but volcanic stones worked great for the purpose.

Our camp was laid out on a broad slope of mixed rock and icy snowbanks on the northerly sheltered side of a ridge. A small, permanent hut perched between the three satellite tents, each spaced about one hundred yards away.

Setting up the sleeping tents was a big part of moving in for occupation, at least initially. In seasons past, rough platforms had been flattened large enough to accommodate a Scott tent, but winter snows had drifted over these platforms and frozen, necessitating a lot of shoveling to carve out space. The shoveling was pleasant work, since it helped me stay warm. It reminded me of digging my ice coffin. Temperatures hovered around fifteen degrees below freezing. Once my tent was ready for occupation, I moved in a pad, sleeping bag, and alarm clock. Pretty much everything else would stay in the warmer hut to keep my stuff from freezing solid.

The hut, otherwise home, stretched to about the dimensions of an elongated McDonald's restroom, nine by fifteen feet. This building was installed a couple decades ago to house scientists working at Crozier. Its walls had been battered by years of wind storms, but stood solid.

"Welcome home." Michelle greeted me with a grin as I patted off loose snow in the doorway. She was stacking piles of metal penguin tags on a high shelf. "First impressions?"

"I like the hiking around here," I said, earnestly. "Good and healthy, all that exercise. But it's nice to come back to four solid walls and a heater."

Kirsten stepped in behind me. "Ah, Crozier," she began. "Like we never left. This place really puts a hold on you after a while."

Inside, the hut was cramped, cluttered, and cozy. It consisted of two main rooms, one for storage and a larger area for occupation. The main space was jammed with a propane heater and stove flanking one corner, a table and three chairs, and four bunks hanging by chains from the ceiling. There was barely space to take three steps down a narrow walkway in between. The storage room held shelves for dry and canned foods, some of which had been there for years.

Settling into a chair and fanning my gloved hands around the heater, I inspected a variety of artwork and curios scattered on walls and shelves by past crews.

On one wall hung a watercolor by accomplished bird artist 81
Sophie Webb, who spent a season at Crozier and subsequently published a children's book about the experience. The painting, depicting an Adélie Penguin at its nest, was kept in place with thumbtacks and electrical tape. Lying around were bits of Emperor Penguin eggshells, stones, lichens, and other natural debris. A thick length of copper wire, little more than a foot long, rested on a shelf—probably an artifact from one of the earliest expeditions to Crozier. A cartoon drawing traced onto a closet door between bunk beds outlined a pile of penguins, each stacked on each other's shoulders in a towering balancing act, while a Leopard Seal looked on with a leer. At the opposite end of the room, on the inside of the entrance door, an Emperor Penguin skin hung like a tiger pelt, stretching almost from knee height

to eye level, giving a close view of the bird's impressive full size. A few books had accumulated from year to year, including an extremely tattered copy of Cherry's book. He probably would appreciate that an edition of his writing had made it back.

Every available surface inside the hut was filled up. Pots and pans hung from improvised nails; various wires snaked across ceiling and walls; shelves bulged with assorted radio chargers, boxes of GPS tags, and nest flags. I'd worked and lived in similar field houses in Oregon, Michigan, Maine, Panama, Ecuador, and a few other places, and happily appraised the cluttered space. A field station is a field station the world over.

Outside, alongside the hut, a lean-to housed additional storage at outdoor temperature. This included all of our frozen food, like meat and veggies, which wouldn't thaw until brought inside. Affixed to the front of the hut was a plywood outhouse complete with door and steps at the entrance. Inside, a hard foam seat rested above enough space to fit a white plastic bucket. Sleds and sections of improvised fencing were strapped to one side of the outhouse, and several propane tanks were secured nearby to a sheltered wall. About fifty yards away stood a shiny metal windmill, recently installed to complement the solar array that powered the hut's various electronics. That windmill, facing into the famous Crozier winds, actually generated too much power, and was usually shut down to prevent shorting out the system.

Kirsten reverently removed the tattered *Worst Journey* book from its shelf. "I brought a replacement this year," she said, and pulled a glossy new copy from her suitcase.

"Cherry lives on," Michelle observed with affection. "Crozier should have a good edition." She finished stacking penguin tags and moved into the storage space to unpack and categorize groceries.

Later, trapped inside the hut during a storm, we would read passages aloud from this book. The harrowing events of that early expedition put our circumstances in proper context.

"Hope we get a real blizzard this year," I mused.

"Better watch what you wish for," Michelle answered.

I looked out a tiny window over the propane stove. The view appeared serene and orderly, pure white snow and ice under blue skies. Even the windmill was still. So far, Crozier was keeping its aggression under wraps.

In the distance, a ridgeline snaked down toward the frozen ocean. Somewhere behind that ridge, a quarter-million penguins were finding mates, tending nests, and going about daily business. Soon enough, I'd be among them.

"Mostly, I can't wait to get out in the penguin colony," I said.

Kirsten and Michelle paused and smiled at each other. As returnees, they each knew exactly what it was like to walk among penguins. This year, they would be visiting old friends.

"That's what we come for," said Michelle.

"That's why we came back," added Kirsten. "Penguins are addictive."

I envisioned the sprawling penguin colony on a busy day, with birds as far as the eye could see, waddling on their tiny legs, bellies distended with fish, recognizing their chicks among the masses. This was a spectacle that most people only ever see on TV. Few get the opportunity to experience it firsthand. "Here, help me sort this bag of old nest flags," said Kirsten.

Time to snap out of my reverie. On the table sat a canvas sack full of yellow cattle tags. Each tag had a distinct identification number inscribed in permanent marker and a nail that could secure it to frozen ground, helping mark individual penguin nests. Most of the old tags were covered in dried, years-old penguin guano.

With a sigh, I dropped into one of the metal chairs and began to sort out usable nest flags. Powdered penguin poo built up on the floor and on my parka, forming the first of many layers of grime.

83

16. Among Penguins

✳✳✳

Think of the biggest rock concert you've ever been to, except everyone is two feet tall, wearing a tuxedo, and smells like fish.

And you're on stage.

I absolutely felt like a rock star entering the penguin colony for the first time. Kirsten, Michelle, and I had stuffed about forty pounds of gear into each of our packs, suited up in cold-weather clothing, and left the hut in late morning after a relaxed breakfast. Conditions couldn't have been more inviting for our first day afield. Sunshine glared off ice fields under calm skies. A brisk forty-five-minute hike, using metal-spiked crampons to grip glimmering blue ice underfoot, led us eventually to a ridgetop, where, on one side, the ground sloped away into ice and nothingness. In front, a valley was packed with more penguins than I could have dreamed existed.

I stood there surrounded, awed, and slightly sickened by my first real sight of penguins. Hundreds, thousands, hundreds of thousands of them. In every direction, curious eyes stared, beaks preened, tails lifted over streaming shots of smelly defecation. Penguins seethed, growled, walked aimlessly in circles. The crowd was overpowering.

Masses of penguins blackened the valley, burnt the landscape, as if a wildfire had left ribbons of writhing, charred ashes on the ice. They trailed off into the horizon, perspective blending the birds into the distant Ross Ice Shelf.

Michelle pointed down-valley to where wide rivers of penguins flowed to meet the frozen ocean. "Let's head down there," she suggested. "That's where most of the action concentrates." She gazed over the kingdom with a confident look. Michelle seemed completely at ease here, in her element, unfazed by the sight of chaos in front of us. She regarded the scene as a biologist on a mission.

But I wasn't quite so calm. "We're completely outnumbered!" I blurted, wide eyed at the sight of penguin armies in full deployment.

Before we could advance or retreat, a greeting party of penguins waddled toward us. Five or six birds hurried on short, stumpy legs as fast as they could go, stopping just short of my boots. One stepped forward, inspected my feet from several inches away, and craned its head upward. It goggled an eye, stared hard, and rolled its pupils, evidently expressing strong emotion, then doubled over and gingerly untied one of my boot laces. That task accomplished, it stepped back and sized me up.

I stared right back. The penguin was the size and shape of a fat bowling pin, patterned with the classic tuxedo—black with a white belly. At full stretch, it reached just above my kneecaps. Strong, fully feathered feet gripped the ice like crampon spikes. The bird's plumage was smartly demarcated, crisp and clean, but I was most taken with the penguin's ever-changing expressions. Pale eyes peered from a dark face, showing curiosity one second, trepidation the next. It was clear that this bird didn't know what to think of us.

Its friends likewise were stymied, and stood in a rough line facing Kirsten, Michelle, and me, unsure of their next move.

Kirsten broke the standoff by stepping confidently sideways to circumvent the dumbstruck penguin gang. "Watch your step," she warned as Michelle and I followed. "The icy spots are slippery and the rocky areas are loose, and look out for eggs."

As we waded knee deep into the valley of penguins, I glanced back over my shoulder. The original greeting party had snapped out of their trance, and, apparently with nothing better to do, followed close on our heels. Other curious penguins joined in, and we soon trailed a gaggle of several dozen birds wobbling quickly to keep pace.

Kirsten threaded a path through the masses of penguins by sticking to open lanes between subcolonies. These bare spaces were used by commuting birds, and we constantly dodged oncoming traffic to stay clear of collisions. Fat penguins, bellies

85

bloated with fish, waddled slowly uphill toward their nests and mates, so intent on their own business that they hardly minded our passage.

The birds harbored little fear of us. This early in the season, a large number of the adults sprawled on nests in a half-asleep state, eyelids drooping, feathers fluffed out. They lay prone on their bellies, facing head on into the wind, each one spaced about three feet from the next, focused on keeping eggs warm. They hardly turned their heads as we passed within several feet.

Other penguins, young and unattached, roamed freely without much agenda. These inexperienced birds were troublemakers, including the entourage following us.

I heard a stifled scream behind me and turned around just in time to face a kamikaze youngster in full charge. The penguin had decided to attack, and rushed on tippy toes, chest puffed out, flippers waving maniacally. It was funny until the moment of impact.

"Ah! Gerroff!" I yelped, as the penguin went toe to toe with my right shin, flipper bashing at my lower leg for all it was worth. "Michelle—Kirsten? These things are feisty!"

After I had nudged it with my foot, the bird finally relented, threw a psychotic look, then flipped around and sprinted away as fast as it had arrived to rejoin a gang of prowling, youthful penguins. My shin definitely hurt. Penguin flippers are stronger than they look. I rubbed bruises through the thick layers of windproofing and long underwear.

"Gotta watch out for the two- and three-year-olds," advised Kirsten. "They return to the colony for the summer, but aren't yet old enough to breed, so they pretty much hang around with nothing to do except fight, flirt, and cause mischief for everyone else. They're just getting the hang of things at this point."

The young birds looked exactly like adults, but their behavior gave them away. In meandering packs they investigated the most unlikely areas, like an ice cliff abutting one side of the valley, for no purpose beyond exploration. Lines of them headed off toward the interior, roaming desolate territory that offered nothing particularly productive for a penguin. There was a sort of kinship in this, and I liked the youngsters. They represented the future.

Kirsten, Michelle, and I continued to pick our way steadily deeper among the throngs of penguins. We stepped, slipped, and switchbacked down a long rock and ice slope toward the floor of the valley, taking care to avoid nests and wandering birds.

At the junction of a perpendicular ridgeline, Michelle separated, heading off in a different direction to check an outlying subcolony in a parallel valley. We coordinated VHF radio frequencies and made dinner plans before splitting up. Her Big Red jacket was visible as a dwindling splotch of color until it fell out of sight behind a penguin-covered fold in terrain. Kirsten and I continued down to the valley floor and eventually reached a flat area near the ocean that was dense with crowded subcolonies.

Kirsten shucked her pack and pulled out a piece of paper. It flapped in a gentle breeze as she held the corners between thick gloves. "We're right here," she said, jabbing an index finger. The paper showed an aerial photograph of the penguin colony. This view was even more exaggerated than my first look from the top of the ridgeline above the valley. On the photo map, penguins were represented as literal specks. Thousands of closely arranged dots formed oddly artistic, swirling patterns.

Individual subcolonies were outlined with black borders on the photo and labeled helpfully with capital letters. "So, we're in Area M now?" I asked, squinting at the map.

"Yep," Kirsten said. "Might as well get used to it. Area M is your territory this season."

17. Area M

✳✳✳

It was difficult at first to relate the photo to the landscape. The little dots didn't connect in my mind to the sprawling masses of penguins, especially when birds kept bumping into my boots. I tried not to get too distracted.

Area M was subdivided into individual subcolonies, which had been assigned unique numbers for convenience. Each isolated subcolony held between twenty and three thousand penguin nests. Most were separated physically by lanes of open space, but a few ran confusingly together like ink blots.

As I glanced back and forth between the aerial photo and the actual penguin colony, Kirsten explained the process of our field work. "Basically, we'll spend 80 percent of our time searching for banded penguins," she said. "In each of the last thirteen years, one thousand baby penguins were marked at Crozier—that makes thirteen thousand banded penguins on the record books. Our job is to census the colony to see which ones survived to return this year."

"What if we miss one?" I wondered.

"Actually," Kirsten clarified, "we look at every single one of those quarter-million penguins once every two weeks. Over the course of two or three months, that means we'll have a pretty good chance of resighting most of the marked birds that visit the colony this summer. And most of the banded penguins live in Area M, where they were originally hatched; very few wander to other regions of the colony. Rarest of all are the birds that were marked at one of the other Ross Island colonies: Cape Bird, Cape Royds, or Beaufort Island. They don't move much between colonies, but it does occasionally happen."

Penguins are typically banded using small metal tags that fit snugly around the armpit of their flippers, like a permanent upper armband. Unique five-digit numbers engraved in the metal identify individuals throughout their lives. The bands never fall off and don't interfere with the birds' activities. The numbers face outward and are large enough to be read through binoculars from a distance. Other types of birds are often ringed with standard leg bands for research purposes, but the unusually short, feathered legs of penguins can become matted and infected underneath such hardware—hence the flipper tags.

"Most penguins return to the same nest year after year," Kirsten continued, "which makes our job easier. Known nests of banded penguins are marked with yellow cattle tags nailed to the ground."

"And how long can a penguin live?" I asked.

Kirsten considered for a moment. "This project is in its thirteenth year," she said, "and we've still got lots of Adélies returning that were marked the first season. They probably live ten to fifteen years, on average. Of course, an Emperor Penguin might survive past age fifty."

Though we wouldn't do much hands-on research with them, several hundred Emperor Penguins also nested at Cape Crozier— the same group that had inspired Cherry-Garrard's adventure— and I'd later have the chance to visit their colony sheltered against a nook in the Ross Ice Shelf.

For now, the tiny Adélies consumed my full attention.

"There—" Kirsten said, and pointed an outstretched, gloved hand. "There's a banded penguin!"

Sure enough, a nearby penguin was differentiated from its neighbors by a shiny metal band on its left flipper. The number was clearly visible: 47501. I grabbed a pencil and wrote these digits in my field notebook along with notes about behavior and location. I also took a GPS reading of the nest site, which could later be mapped in a computer program. Once this observation was entered into a database on the laptop in our hut, I'd be able to bring up the bird's complete history.

"It's easy to tell if a bird is banded," Kirsten said. "They're all marked on the left flipper, so you don't have to check both sides.

And since most of the birds face the wind when they sit on their nests, they're often all pointed in the same direction."

We meandered along the edge of a subcolony, visually sifting through crowds of penguins to search for marked birds.

"Hey, I see one!" I exclaimed. This penguin was on a nest next to a yellow cattle flag that had been nailed into the hard ground the previous year, indicating the bird had returned to exactly the same spot one year later.

Searching for banded penguins was a little like scanning for needles in a haystack, but to discover one was immensely satisfying. "Gotcha," I muttered as I wrote in my field notebook. "You can't hide from this penguin searcher!"

"Looking for marked penguins is an endurance activity," Kirsten said. "You might be wandering out here eight hours a day, usually alone. I think it's pretty Zen, sometimes, just sifting penguins, like you can just zone out and reach some kind of different level of meaning with all these birds around you. You'll figure out your own methods, though."

I couldn't believe this was my job: staring at penguins. It still seemed too incredible to be true.

Michelle's voice crackled through the VHF radio. "Hey, guys, can you hear me?" She used a line-of-sight channel, which didn't require much formality. Other radio channels were bounced off a repeater unit on Mount Terror and could be heard at McMurdo Station on the other side of Ross Island. The radio was our safety net in case of emergency.

"Never better," Kirsten replied.

"How are the penguins looking?" Michelle's voice inquired.

"Very friendly," said Kirsten. "Just like we never left."

"OK, just making sure the radio works," Michelle said and signed off.

Kirsten and I decided to split up for a couple hours to begin the season's search for banded penguins. While she hiked to a different group of subcolonies about a mile away, out of sight around a corner at the other end of the valley, I slowly began to cover Area M, frequently referencing the photo map.

Soon, I was alone with the penguins.

18. Metropolis

✳✳✳

Male Adélie Penguins, differentiated from females by their slightly larger size, thicker beaks, and bulkier heads, were in charge of claiming and defending nest territories. They'd pick a spot, scratch out a small depression in the ground, and stand over it protectively. Every now and then, the males proclaimed their existence with a loud, trumpeting, guttural, chanting call, directed at the sky.

To customize their nest, these penguins gathered tiny pebbles and arranged them, with utmost care, into a bowl-shaped platform. In some spots, stones were thin on the ground. Most were frozen in or had been blown away on the wind, so competition was fierce for the best pebbles.

I watched with fascination as two neighboring single male penguins in Area M waged a protracted war over nest stones. Each had gathered about the same number of quality rocks for his own nest, but both birds obviously wanted more, and none were within easy reach. When a wandering female distracted one bird, the second male took the opportunity to reach over and steal a good stone. The thief turned his back to spy on another penguin's cache, and then the first bird stole his rock back. There ensued a spirited pecking battle over the disputed burglary. This went on endlessly.

Up and down long, narrow subcolonies of penguins, I wandered methodically, visually sifting through the birds to pick out banded individuals. It was slightly voyeuristic to watch the penguins go about their day-to-day business, like peeking through the windows of a hotel.

Males and females, once paired, took turns incubating eggs while their mates went out to sea for food. Penguins with eggs sat horizontally on their nests, entirely at rest, eyelids half closed, in a semi-catatonic state. What went through their minds during the long days of incubation? Perhaps the penguins dreamed of future adventures, relived past highlights, or thought of nothing at all.

In twenty-four-hour sunshine, it didn't matter when the birds slept, so they caught power naps whenever needed. Some areas were clearly popular for napping, since flotillas of penguins could be reliably found sleeping there. Many birds rested near the edge of land after returning from a feeding trip to the ocean, and I took extra care not to awaken slumbering penguins as I tiptoed past.

Individual penguins constantly commuted between the penguin colony and the ocean. This early in the season, the birds had to walk for miles across frozen water to enter the sea. Long lines of waddling penguins were visible slowly wobbling toward the horizon until they were too small to see with the unaided eye. At a distance, the upright silhouettes were startlingly human in character, like refugees straggling over a frozen border.

Every now and then, I stumbled across a banded bird and jotted its details in my field notebook: how many eggs it was incubating, where its nest was located, date and time. To keep disturbance to a minimum, I often waited several minutes for an incubating bird to shift positions to see how many eggs it was sitting on, rather than pushing the penguin off its nest. I also GPSed nests of numbered penguins so they could later be plotted on a map. Over seasons' worth of observations, this information could be used to analyze a wide variety of population dynamics.

Within the colony, it was easy to tell which birds had just returned from a feeding trip. When penguins arrived after several days at sea, the water had washed off all dirt and their plumage shone beautifully clean, with bellies as white as a bleached tablecloth. Birds that had been tending their nests, by contrast, could be distinguished by dingy bellies stained with guano and dirt. Some, who had chosen poor nest sites, became covered in blackish frozen mud.

In their general state of grunginess, it was difficult for me to get clean photographs of penguins. There was always something dirty in the frame, wherever I pointed the camera. The ice looked clean, but the penguins rarely were. Photographing penguins in the metropolis was at once ridiculously easy and frustrating. My 300mm lens gave too much magnification, so I was forever backing up, while my penguin subjects followed me around, and we chased each other around the colony. My batteries also froze quickly, and I had to carry two spares and charge them every night.

Around the colony, dead penguins did not rot as they would in warmer climates. Accordingly, bodies of unfortunate birds piled up from one season to the next, dispersed only by skuas, which carried off edible bits, or the wind. Many carcasses mummified into a dry, near-skeletal state, hardened into the earth and ice. Penguin mummies covered a lot of the ground surface. Research has indicated that at least some of them are hundreds or even thousands of years old.

Handy penguins sometimes used pieces of carcasses as nest stones. A male tried to woo a passing female with the severed vertebra of a long-dead chick while a nearby penguin padded his nest with skulls and wing bones. Several nest platforms were built on top of mummified penguins, with frozen bodies as supports. To the practical birds, death was an abstract concept. Once dead, a carcass lacked any special significance. If the bones could be used productively, the penguins harbored no qualms in doing so.

South Polar Skuas patrolled the colony, looking for any chance to steal penguin eggs. Sometimes several skuas would gang up on an unfortunate penguin parent to lure it away from its eggs, but, more often, the predators darted in while a penguin wasn't paying attention.

It was painful to watch penguins lose their eggs. Skuas preyed most on nests close to the edge of individual subcolonies that were not completely insulated by neighboring penguins. These birds, likely young and inexperienced, were doomed to failure, but I cheered for them anyway.

When one skua swiped a penguin's egg in mid-flight, the parent turned around in agitation. It had no eggs left, and would not

93

re-nest until the following year. There was nothing for the bird to do. The penguin slowly wandered away from its empty nest, suddenly purposeless. Soon, other penguins had stolen all of the nest stones.

For each egg the skuas stole, though, hundreds more were carefully guarded by alert parents, and the colony bustled with activity. Penguins thronged around as I searched for banded birds. Aggressive ones pressed in, pushed closer by nudges from behind, until I was at the center of a curious, staring crowd. Some of the penguins tired quickly of me and wandered off. Others followed along behind me.

I hit the transmit button on my radio. "Michelle, I'm a rock star!" I announced.

"Repeat that?" returned a confused, static-filled reply. Michelle was now working on the other side of a tall ridge, half a mile away, at the limit of the line-of-sight radio channel.

"Never mind."

I wasn't really looking for a response. My fans were all around me. Groupies, paparazzi, and curious onlookers—they were all here. Cut off from the world, I nonetheless entertained a crowd. In the most remote place on Earth, I stalked a metropolis. Nowhere could I have felt more at home.

19. Man Hauling

❄❄❄

"Let's pack it up," Michelle said.

All three of us struggled into cold weather clothing, arranged our packs, and headed outdoors.

Our project for the second day at Crozier involved encircling a small subcolony of nesting penguins inside a plastic fence with only one entrance. The penguins, once they located the entrance, would commute back and forth to their nests over the same patch of ground. At this spot, the penguins waddled over a scale. Certain birds were marked with tiny PIT (Passive Integrated Transponder) tags implanted in their flippers, which could be used to identify them as they were electronically scanned. The data were stored on a computer. By measuring how much weight the birds gained on each feeding trip, once every one to three days, we could tell how much food they were eating, and we could compare single birds against each other.

First, the fencing and equipment had to be moved to the site and set up.

For gear too heavy to haul in a backpack, we used a large sled, just like early Antarctic explorers. For lack of sled dogs, Kirsten, Michelle, and I would pull the weight ourselves.

I undid the cargo straps attaching the sled to the side of our outhouse and positioned it on the snow in front of the hut. Michelle and Kirsten worked together to extract equipment from our storeroom and arrange it on the sled.

The heaviest object was an eighty-pound battery encased in a plywood box. This went into the sled first, right in the middle. Several rolls of heavy plastic fencing were piled on, as well as a tent, solar panels, shovels, and other tools, secured with straps and ropes. The whole contraption weighed several hundred pounds.

We attached three harnesses to the front of the sled. Each of us secured crampons to our boots, shouldered packs full of personal gear, food, and water, and tied into separate harnesses.

"Thank goodness it's downhill all the way to the penguin colony," I breathed. Between our camp and the penguins lay an ice slope stretching about one mile.

The hardest part of sledging was getting up momentum. The wooden sled stuck to the ice with the weight of all its cargo, and we leaned into our traces, pulling mightily to get it moving. Once unstuck, the sled picked up speed rapidly downslope, threatening to rumble out of control. Two of us shifted around to the back end to brake, digging in with our crampons on the hard ice.

Steering the sled presented no problem. The hauler in front pulled left or right as terrain dictated. Though the ice slope angled evenly downhill, it was crossed by treacherous sastrugi—wind-sculpted ridges of packed snow. These ridges, one to three feet high and hard as rock, swept across the valley in line with prevailing breezes, offering us a variety of inclines like the choppy surfaces of a windy ocean. Sometimes we navigated around sheer faces and undercut mini-cornices. The sled bumped over each ridge, requiring a hard pull up one side and a quick braked descent on steep spots.

It was tough sledding. I soon dripped with sweat under my thick parka. "Glad this isn't our main form of transportation," I gasped.

"Could be worse," Kirsten pointed out. "Imagine doing this in seventy below, total darkness, and through crevasse fields, like Cherry-Garrard and his crew on their way to Crozier in the early 1900s."

I was glad we didn't have to worry about crevasses. The ice slope we traversed was relatively small for a glacier and entirely concave. Crevasses generally form when ice slides over a convex surface. Think of bending a Snickers bar over your index finger, with little cracks in the chocolate representing crevasses. When such cracks develop in a large glacier, thin snow bridges often cover the top, obscuring the danger.

Inside the U.S. Air Force C-17 to McMurdo Station.

Deplaning on the frozen surface of the Ross Sea.

Ivan the Terrabus (left) and two Delta shuttles stand ready to transport passengers.

Happy Campers try to stay warm during a survival exercise.

Antarctica's dry and wind-packed snow is perfect for quarrying blocks.

A National Science Foundation helicopter whips spindrift while landing at Cape Crozier.

The Crozier field camp includes a permanent hut and three canvas sleeping tents.

The nine-by-fifteen-foot Crozier hut (with attached outhouse).

Adult Adélie Penguin.

A curious marching band of young penguins.

Kirsten Lindquist pauses, ice axe in hand, at the edge of the Ross Ice Shelf.

Kirsten (left) and Michelle (right) follow a distant Snow Petrel.

Michelle Hester fills
out a penguin nest flag.

Adult Emperor Penguins.

A slow-moving Emperor Penguin is thronged by passing Adélies.

Noah is surrounded, as usual, by curious penguins.

Young Emperor
Penguins look
like kids in their
grandmas' Christmas
sweaters.

Very young
Adélie Penguins
stick together for
warmth.

Noah wrangles a young penguin.

In late summer, the Ross Sea thaws enough to break up sea ice.

Adélie Penguins dive from a fantastic abutment of icicles formed by freezing sea spray.

Like dolphins, Adélie Penguins porpoise for air while swimming.

A Weddell Seal
lounges on the
ice.

A Snow Petrel knifes by the
summit of Pat's Peak.

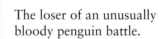

The loser of an unusually
bloody penguin battle.

South Polar Skuas typically eat fish, but a few have learned to rip the stomachs out of baby Adélie Penguins.

Noah's tent after two days of hurricane-force winds.

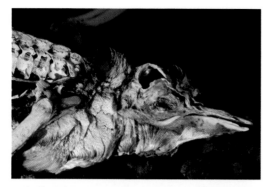

Mummified carcasses, some hundreds or thousands of years old, crunch underfoot in the penguin colony.

Blondie sits on his nest.

Blackie relaxes.

Noah in the valley of penguins.

Flipper tags help
scientists keep track
of individual birds.

The penguin roundup: researchers corral young birds between two sections of plastic fencing for banding.

A lenticular cloud over the penguin colony signals windy weather ahead.

top left: Noah, before traveling to Antarctica.

top right: Mid-season in Antarctica.

right: At the end of the Antarctica field season.

Man Hauling

✳

Just north of McMurdo Station, crevasses in the Erebus Glacier Tongue form ice caves as the glacier flows into the Ross Sea. With a solid floor, these caves tunnel far into the ice. In the unique formations, it's possible to safely explore crevasses at ground level.

I'd visited the ice caves in my sea ice-safety class during gear-up in McMurdo Station. The outing was the highlight of two days of survival training. Class had finished early in the afternoon, so we had some free time. We were still talking about the morning's single penguin sighting when Matt, our instructor, offered another adventure.

"Hey, anyone want to explore some ice caves?" Hands went up all around. Matt grinned. "OK, let's go," he said. "Everyone in the Hagglund!"

A dozen of us climbed into the specialized tracked vehicle, our transportation on the ice. It resembled a rectangular red tank with narrow windows, and the name "Gretel" was stenciled on the front.

Matt drove us straight across the frozen surface of the Ross Sea. We'd traveled about twenty miles from McMurdo Station over the course of the day, wandering in search of different ice features, like cracks and grounded icebergs, and learning about the effects of currents, wind, and temperature on ice thickness.

Navigating over the sea ice was surreal. It seemed to be a continuous, flat expanse, like an ocean that had been flash frozen. In some places, there was even a suggestion of waves, though these were caused by the wind after freezing. Several rocky islands poked through, giving the only suggestion of land underneath the ice.

Here and there were scattered diver's huts. Experienced scuba divers used these as entryways to the eerie, watery world underneath the ice. The huts resembled fishermen's shacks. A hole would be carved in the icy floor, and one diver would go down on a tether while his buddy remained topside, stirring the hole to keep it from refreezing. Matt explained that the BBC was using one set of huts to film a television documentary about the ocean's wildlife.

Gretel, our Hagglund, drew up to a long, steep ridge in the ice, and Matt stopped the vehicle. From the driver's seat, he pointed at a dark spot on the cliff face. "That's the entrance to the caves," he said. "Ready to explore?"

Our group hopped out and approached the cliffs. Matt led the way confidently.

The cave looked like a crevasse that had formed higher in the Erebus Glacier before twisting into a sealed passageway when the glacier crunched into the sea. The entrance was a small, roughly circular hole about four feet wide in a vertical section of cliff.

"Follow me!" Matt said. He jumped into the hole and abruptly disappeared.

"Where did he go?" a mechanic asked.

I leaned into the cave, and, in its half light, couldn't see Matt. "Looks like a trip," I said. "Guess I'll trust him." Without a trace of caution, I jumped into the hole.

The cave formed a narrow tunnel. I landed on my butt and started sliding downhill into its depths. Walls and ceiling closed in as I scooted downward until I shot along in a smooth passage. I had to lean back as the roof closed down. It was like a twisting ride from an amusement park without knowing where it ended. With solid ice on all sides, dim sunlight cast a bluish tint.

Suddenly, the passageway opened into a large cavern, and the grade adjusted to a flat floor. I slid to a stop and stood up, dusting ice flakes off my jacket.

Matt stood expectantly in the cavern.

"Whew!" I exclaimed. "That was a rush!"

"It's like an ice cathedral," he said, gesturing at the cave's interior.

Walls of ice wedged in at smooth, geometric angles like something from a modern designer's fantasy. Everything glittered in a deep blue, dusky light. Pillars and fantastic shapes filled the cave. Crystals of ice swept from floor to ceiling. Jumbled slabs of ice formed a roof forty feet overhead.

Deep in the glacier, sunlight penetrated through tortuous cracks, refracting off angled surfaces and absorbing through thick, frozen layers. Darker areas were cast in deep blue shadows, and lighter areas shone with a brilliant white radiance. In between, colors transitioned through soft gradients.

Gradually, each of the dozen members of the sea ice safety course popped through the entrance chute. We walked on a narrow, flat floor deeper into the cave, marveling at its features. After a hundred yards, the floor ended in a solid, vertical wall of ice. "End of the line," said Matt.

"This is just incredible," marveled a volcanic scientist.

"Yeah," agreed the mechanic. "I was in a so-called 'ice cave' once in northern California, but that was just a rocky cave that was cold enough to form ice in its depths. This one is made entirely out of ice!"

"Are we still spelunkers if the cave isn't made of rock?" another man wondered.

Matt laughed. "Well, these cave systems shift every year as the glacier advances," he said. "This is a completely different arrangement than last year."

"So, it's like the Ice Hotel," the scientist said. "It changes every summer."

The Ice Hotel was an apt comparison. Every winter, artistic engineers design a luxury hotel north of the Arctic Circle in Lapland, Sweden, built completely of ice. When spring comes, the building melts. The next winter, a new design is constructed. These ice caves in Antarctica were nearly as ephemeral, since they shifted with the glacier's movements, but were designed entirely by natural forces.

Deep inside the ice, the isolation was palpable. Not even radio signals could reach through these walls. Sound, wind, and light were buffered. I thought about the thousands of mountain climbers and explorers who have died over the centuries after falling in crevasses, and shivered. It would be a long, slow, agonizingly lonely death, trapped below the frozen ground. Glad to return to open air, I picked my way up the narrow entrance tunnel, carefully placing each step to avoid slipping on the ice.

"Let's aim over that way," Michelle suggested, indicating a roundabout path avoiding an area of potholed ice.

The three of us pulled in our traces and dragged the sled across a flat area. Sometimes we hit a rhythm and marched smoothly along. At other times, our steps were misaligned and the sled jerked forward. It was tough to gauge our progress along the icy surface when each step looked the same. Without many landmarks, I hadn't realized how fast we traveled. When we came around the corner, I was surprised to see the edge of the penguin colony just a hundred yards ahead. Our hut had disappeared behind us in a fold in snowy terrain.

The experimental subcolony was separated from the rest of the penguins by a band of open, rocky ground, so it was possible to see which birds were to be fenced in. Metal posts had been pounded already into the ground to hold the plastic fencing. But snow had drifted throughout the winter, and in some places it was three feet high where the fence should be.

"Guess we're going to be doing a lot of shoveling," Kirsten said.

I cracked a smile. "I'll do it," I volunteered. "I'm getting pretty good at shoveling snow."

"Happy camping, installing tents, and now clearing fences," Michelle said. "It's good to have someone who likes to shovel."

"All right," Kirsten said. "Michelle and I can start installing the weighbridge setup while you get going on the fence."

The scale and scanners were rolled into one giant weather-resistant package of electronics called a "weighbridge," designed like a drawbridge that weighed its traffic. This one was specially designed for penguins.

We gratefully unhitched ourselves from the sled and got to work. I put on my Big Red, which I'd removed halfway down the hill, when sweat started freezing to my skin. A few minutes later, I took off the jacket again. Shoveling snow kept me plenty warm. I juggled a constant balance of clothing layers and body heat.

The subcolony was roughly circular and contained a few dozen penguin nests. The fence skirted around the perimeter, forming a circle twenty or thirty yards wide. Where the fence line went, I dug a trench through several feet of snow to ground level.

Kirsten began bolting two solar panels to a piece of secure plywood while Michelle set up a mountain tent next to the weighbridge entrance. The tent would hold the large battery, computer, and other more sensitive electronics to support the weighbridge, as well as an extra sleeping bag and pad in case we became stranded here during a storm.

Digging my way around the fence line, I suddenly realized that one penguin had decided to nest right where the fence should go. We had a problem.

20. Life of a Penguin

❄❄❄

By the time an Adélie Penguin hatches from its egg, it's already covered with a fine layer of gray fuzz. The hatchling, resembling a dainty Beanie Baby, is barely strong enough to lift its head or open its eyes, and can't maintain its own body temperature. The young penguin has one sibling, and they hatch within a day of each other, vying for position in the nest beneath the soft folds of a parent's belly to stay warm. Typically, one of the siblings won't make it past the first short months of life.

The baby penguin's world is defined by unyielding features. Its nest forms a bowl-shaped scrape in frozen soil lined with loose pebbles and other debris. Within a one-meter radius, several other penguins attend their own chicks. Beyond, snow, ice, and rock blend into a white horizon.

Every now and then, one of the chick's parents tenderly barfs up a heady concoction of half-digested krill and fish parts. The baby penguin takes the offering by cramming its head halfway down its parent's throat, ensuring that not a drop of the stuff is wasted during transfer.

Parents come and go, switching duties at the nest at regular intervals. While one watches the chicks, the other goes to sea to find food under the ice. When a skua, penguin, or human approaches the nest too closely, the parent attempts to peck the trespasser into submission. Otherwise, the adult penguin relaxes in a state of half-awake boredom.

Soon, though, the chick is big enough to stay warm on its own. Half the size of its parent, it has a thick coat of fluffy, downy feathers. Without fanfare, both parents leave their chicks alone on shore. The young penguin wanders from its nest for the first time to join a dense huddle with a dozen neighboring chicks. When a parent returns with food, once every day or two, it recognizes the voices of its own chicks among the sea of lookalikes. Though gangs of half-grown penguins chase after it in hopes of stealing a meal, the adult will feed only its own young. This pattern continues for a few weeks until, toward the end of summer, the parents abandon their children ashore for the last time. Now, the penguin chick must fend for itself.

Gradually, the chick loses its coat of fluff, transforming into a sleek, adult-like bird. One day, as the sun begins to dip toward the horizon, it waddles to the edge of the ocean, wades into the water, and swims to sea.

It spends the next three or four years living a nomadic existence among the pack ice, learning to survive the brutal Antarctic winters, dodging Leopard Seals, and catching lots of fish. For the first year, it is recognizable by a white throat. After that, the young penguin is, by all appearances, an adult.

Assuming the penguin is still alive, it returns to land at age three or four, probably to the same part of the same colony where it hatched. That first summer, the penguin will just hang out, flirt with other penguins, try staking out a territory, and watch from the fringes. The following breeding season, it will find a mate, build a nest, and settle in to family life. If all goes well, it will have two smooth, snowy-white eggs of its own.

The penguin spends the rest of its winters among pack ice and returns to land to raise a new brood each summer. If it lives to old age, the penguin might survive for about fifteen years.

Most penguins die at sea, and their bodies disappear in the giant expanse of ocean. A few adults perish on land, leaving their bones to freeze and mummify among the rocks. Some are eaten by Leopard Seals. Others wander too far in the wrong direction for inexplicable reasons, lost forever in the endless expanses of ice. Eager, younger birds are quick to take over lost territories, and the cycle continues relentlessly from one generation to the next.

21. Wrangling

❆❆❆

"Hey, Kirsten," I called. "Do we have to move the fence?"

A penguin sat on its eggs between two metal poles, exactly where we planned to stretch a section of plastic fencing.

Kirsten paused, a solar panel in one hand. "Hm," she said, considering. "I dunno. Michelle, what do you think?"

We stood a few yards from the penguin in a staring match. The bird seemed nonplussed by the extra attention. Michelle thought, and observed, and came to a conclusion. "I think we can try to move its nest," she said.

Kirsten and I immediately caught on to the idea. If we shifted the rocks and eggs a foot and a half to one side, the penguin would no longer be in the way of the fence. "OK," Kirsten replied. "But if it gets stressed by the move, we'll put it right back and try to move the fence instead."

"Noah, this is a good chance for you to see how to handle a penguin," Michelle added. "We'll be wrangling a bunch of them this season, so watch carefully."

I liked the sound of penguin wrangling. The word flashed a brief, ridiculous image of a cowboy rounding up a herd of penguins while they scattered among Great Basin sagebrush. I figured it would be like herding cats.

Kirsten, though, knew her business. She slowly approached the penguin in a half crouch. When she was within two feet of the bird, it stood up to defend its nest, and things happened fast.

In one motion, Kirsten grabbed the penguin's feet with her left hand, up underneath the belly, and secured her right hand over the base of the tail. With a firm grasp on the bird, she lifted it up and against her body. The penguin's head went into her armpit while its body was supported by Kirsten's left forearm, and its feet were held in her left hand. In this hold, Kirsten perfectly cradled the ten-pound penguin, like a baby, with its head tucked securely into a dark, soft place. While Kirsten held the penguin, Michelle moved in and quickly rearranged its nest and eggs about eighteen inches outside the fence line. This particular penguin was probably a young bird, new to the colony, and would have been a low priority inside the experimental fenced area. The move took just a few seconds.

Kirsten released the penguin. It waddled straight to the eggs and plunked back down to incubate. Then it started reorganizing its nest stones, ignoring us completely.

"Guess I messed up its arrangement," Michelle said with a wry smile.

"Looks like it's pretty happy in the new spot," Kirsten replied. "In fact, I'm not sure it even knows it was moved."

The penguin was still incubating its eggs there until they hatched, weeks later.

I returned to shoveling, and, two hours later, finished clearing the snow from the fence line. Then I unrolled several long sections of plastic fencing and attached them to the metal poles with zip ties. When this was done, the weighbridge presented the only entrance and exit to the subcolony.

Michelle constructed a short ramp of rocks to approach this entrance, then set the weighbridge scale into place. Kirsten hooked it up to the solar panels and battery, and the contraption was ready.

The three of us stood back and watched.

A penguin waddled uphill with clean plumage and a fat belly—sure signs of a bird fresh from a feeding trip. We waited. When it arrived at the fenced-in subcolony, the bird didn't even pause before walking confidently over the weighbridge to reach its nest. The scale took its weight and the scanner read the chip that had been implanted in its wing during a previous season. We exchanged high fives. The weighbridge had been christened into action.

Standing around, though, was getting extremely cold. Clouds blotted out the sun, diffusing contrasts and losing definition on the ice. The temperature, with wind chill, hovered around minus thirty-nine degrees Celsius (without wind chill, it was merely minus fifteen). My toes were numb inside my boots, and sweat had frozen on my skin despite the Big Red. My body was so cold that my stomach turned in knots. I was nauseated.

We'd spent six hours setting up the fence and weighbridge. It was time to head for home. We packed a few tools on the sled, tied in to our harnesses, and hauled it back up the hill. The going was much smoother with less weight. Kirsten, Michelle, and I spread out in a line to haul the sled three abreast. Within minutes, circulation returned like wildfire to my toes, but I was glad for the feeling, even if painful.

As the season wore on, penguins would sleep on the weighbridge, skuas would cover the tent in guano, wind would tear holes in the fabric, and the fence would develop holes. But the equipment would endure. Data were being recorded twenty-four hours a day.

It was a tiring and thoroughly satisfying day's work. The set of precise observations from the weighbridge might help humankind learn just a little more about our penguin friends down south. And I had earned my share of the hot and spicy pasta dinner that Michelle cooked—not to mention the hot chocolate that followed.

22. Penguin Science

Despite their far-flung stomping grounds, Adélie Penguins rank among the most-studied birds on Earth. Charisma, fearlessness, site loyalty, and abundance place them among an elite few species with so-called star appeal that are relatively easy to observe.

People have been studying penguins at Cape Crozier for decades. These birds are better known than most North American species. But we still have a lot to learn. With climate change topping the priorities of today's science, researchers are now focused on the effects of melting ice at Earth's poles, and penguins are caught in the middle of one of the hottest political topics of this millennium.

The press is focused on gloom-and-doom aspects of climate change, citing disappearing Adélie Penguin colonies on the northern Antarctic Peninsula (below South America) as evidence of impending disaster. For instance, a recent feature article in *The New Yorker* magazine profiled a colony of Adélies on Litchfield Island that has shrunk from nine hundred pairs in the 1970s to just five pairs today. That seems bad, but, over the same time period, the Adélie colony at Cape Crozier—now at one hundred and thirty thousand breeding pairs, more than a hundred times larger than the colony spotlighted in *The New Yorker*—has increased by almost 3 percent, and the other Ross Sea colonies (Cape Bird, Cape Royds, and Beaufort Island) have also increased. Penguins may be declining at the northern fringes of their range, but business is booming farther south. Clearly, complex factors are at work.

Climate change wasn't such a hot topic when William Sladen, now a professor emeritus at Johns Hopkins Medical Institutions, set up the first Adélie Penguin study at Cape Crozier in 1959. For ten years, Sladen returned each summer season to band chicks, observe penguins, and collect data on the Crozier Adélie colony, eventually filming a documentary called *Penguin City* there in 1970, which aired on CBC and BBC television.

In the 1960s, Sladen hosted a visiting birder at Cape Crozier named Roger Tory Peterson. The researcher remembers, "His first day out with the Adélies, [Peterson] humiliated us all by saying, 'By the way, did you see that Dominican Gull on the beach?' No—we had NEVER seen one before!" Today, of course, Peterson, thanks to his revolutionary field guides, is remembered as possibly the greatest birder and bird ambassador of all time.

Sladen is likewise well respected after a long career in ornithology. Pushing ninety years old, he continues to study birds, most recently trying to teach migration routes to endangered cranes. His penguin work ended in 1970, but Sladen's star graduate student, David Ainley, picked up the Crozier study soon afterward. By all accounts a sort of bird visionary, Ainley has been tenaciously researching penguins in the Ross Sea area ever since. The current research effort is embodied by the PenguinScience project, a three-way collaboration between Ainley (backed by H. T. Harvey & Associates, an ecological consulting organization), Grant Ballard (representing Point Reyes Bird Observatory), and Katie Dugger (from Oregon State University), funded by the National Science Foundation and made possible by the U.S. Antarctic Program. The three major scientists bring in backup, including people like me, to cover everyday field work.

Consistent, annual presence at penguin colonies around the Ross Sea has proved to be a productive way to conduct research. Rather than providing a narrow snapshot of penguin life and behavior, these scientists are uncovering a long-term picture rife with mini-dramas and annual swings. After almost sixty consecutive years of study at Crozier, today's investigations are framed against a solid background of knowledge.

For instance, when a giant, 165-kilometer-long pair of icebergs lodged against Cape Crozier in 2001, scientists seized the chance to observe the effects of a large-scale natural experiment: What happens when penguins are faced with adverse circumstances?

108

"Even to the degree of being contrary to their usual philopatric behavior," Ainley says, "when faced with conditions not conducive to their well being, they move." In other words, penguins have the ability to adapt. When the icebergs hit, reproductive success plummeted to nearly zero at Crozier. After the bergs finally dissipated two years later, the nearby colony at Cape Royds recorded many birds originally banded at Crozier that had emigrated to find better territories. When faced with major environmental disturbance, some penguins moved to new areas, despite their propensity to return to the old breeding places. And when the icebergs disappeared, breeding success returned to normal at Crozier, showing that the remaining penguins could deal with the disturbance without serious long-term effects.

Ongoing observations have also shown that Ross Sea penguin populations dramatically increased in the early 1980s. Nobody is quite sure why, but wind patterns might have something to do with it. Warming in mid-latitude oceans caused increased velocity and duration of winds around Ross Island over the same time period. It's possible that the stronger winds, by blowing ice away from shore, have kept a polynya—an area of ice-free water— open more reliably, giving penguins access to food and migration routes. In the early part of the breeding season in November, the birds must walk from their nests to the edge of open water, sometimes many miles round trip, across the sea ice. The birds nest on solid land, which in November is surrounded by frozen ocean; the sea ice thaws as summer progresses.

Increased wind may be a local effect of global warming that has indirectly benefited penguins. Before celebrating too much, though, consider that the polynya effect might have already plateaued, since access to open water, once opened, is not affected by further increases in wind. Meanwhile, Antarctic snowstorms are becoming more frequent, accumulating snow in the few areas of bare rock where Adélies can nest. And warmer temperatures are chipping away at Antarctica's ice, the very foundation of its continental systems. Soon, the Ross Sea—which contains less than 10 percent of the global Adélie population—might be one of the last areas of the Southern Ocean with a significant amount of sea ice.

It's clear that penguins are more adaptive than people thought, and that, at the moment, Adélie populations are all right. However, global warming threatens to melt Antarctica's ice at an unprecedented rate. Penguins, dependent on those same icy systems, could become major indicators of climate shifts. For this reason, Ainley calls them "bellwethers of climate change."

"With rising sea levels, the folks in Florida, Wall Street, and other low-lying areas should heed [the penguins'] warning about moving to solid ground," he says. "When nothing is constant, it's your ability to adapt that counts." Leave it to an ornithologist to compare Wall Street executives to Adélie Penguins. But Ainley has a point, and it's backed by decades of research and experience.

As for adapting to Antarctica's conditions, I was doing just fine. Within days of settling at the Crozier field camp, my days were becoming routine.

23. Schedule

✳✳✳

The toughest part of sleeping in a cold tent was getting up in the morning. I struggled with it.

Initially, I stripped down each evening, dancing heroically inside the confines of my tent to change underclothes and slide into my sleeping bag, huddling there for half an hour to warm back up before drifting off to sleep. But this process made waking up even harder. The thought of exiting my warm bag in the morning, donning cold outer layers, and hightailing it out onto the ice was almost too much to bear, especially when the wind kicked up.

So within a week I scrapped my dignity, cleanliness, and general routine, and simply wormed into my sleeping bag still wearing every piece of clothing, including bulky jacket, pants, hat, neck gaiter, and gloves. In the morning, all I had to do was wrestle on my frozen boots and head out the door flap. It was a revelation. Sleeping was admittedly more cramped, jammed tight as a mummy, but it became a hundred times easier to face getting up.

One side effect of this strategy was that I almost never changed clothes. Since showers were unavailable, there wasn't a forced opportunity to strip down. At first, I tried to maintain a schedule—every five days change my underwear, every ten days my T-shirt—but, without actually writing it down, it was just too hard to keep track, especially since we never really knew what day of the week it was. When one day I realized my underwear hadn't been changed in five weeks, things became serious. I hauled out our limited soap supply and washed them with melted snow water. The laundry didn't make much difference; the permeating smell of penguin guano overwhelmed everything anyway.

One morning, Michelle, Kirsten, and I discussed our sleeping arrangements over breakfast. "Ice doesn't make the greatest mattress," said Michelle, stretching out her stiff back as she entered the hut's doorway, sunlight streaming in behind her.

Kirsten grinned. "Just think of it as a water bed. A really cold one." She tended a pot of boiling water on the propane stove, looking typically crisp in clean polar fleece.

"My inflatable sleeping pad is sinking into solid ice," I put in, sympathizing with Michelle. "Every night my body temperature warms a bit of snow underneath, which quickly refreezes. It's like a slow-motion flood. The lake keeps expanding."

Michelle sat down on a metal folding chair and rubbed her eyes. "Well, the ice under my tent is layered on top of solid rock. A flood might be nice once in a while."

I looked from my cereal bowl to Kirsten. "How do you do it?" I wondered. "How do you sleep so comfortably every night?"

It was obvious from her chipper expression each morning and general tidiness that Kirsten had figured out a sustainable evening routine. Even though I had been sleeping like a brick, it was the slumber of exhaustion rather than comfort. I prided myself on being able to drift off anywhere, but I couldn't compare my Antarctic arrangement to a real bed with sheets.

112 "To start with," Kirsten said, with a smile, "I strip down to cozy inner layers before climbing in my sleeping bag." We'd been over this before. I wouldn't budge on my mummified plans. To each his or her own. "And wash my hair once in a while," she continued, still grinning.

I ran a hand through my own matted, greasy scalp. "Yeah, well, you've got more of it," I said. "You should just cut it short, like me. Then you'd never have to wash it. Use less shampoo that way." And I returned to my cereal, trying not to dribble milk down my lengthening beard.

❋

More than anything, I enjoyed breakfast. The thought of it rousted me out of my tent when cold conspired to pin me in my sleeping bag. I would wake up, shake the ice off my hat and sleeping bag where my breath had frozen overnight, put on my boots, and run to the hut to eat. A solid breakfast is the best way to start the day.

Of the usual breakfast items—bacon, eggs, toast, pancakes, cereal, oatmeal—we could cook most in our field hut, with a few twists and exceptions. Isolation and climate put some restrictions on our diet.

Eggs, for instance, were difficult. Real eggs couldn't be frozen or kept in a warm place. Without a refrigerator, we kept a carton of frozen egg substitute outside, next to the meat, on ice. The carton, which resembled a waxed orange juice container, weighed five pounds. Basically, it was a frozen egg brick.

At first, I feared the faux egg brick. It was intimidating. It could kill people if you dropped it on their heads or forced them to eat the entire thing at once. Ancient civilizations might have tortured prisoners with 2.25-kilogram boxes of Rose Acre Fat Free Cholesterol Free Pasteurized Homogenized Frozen Egg Substitute. To cook one egg, you had to take on the whole carton, which was equivalent to more than fifty eggs, in a sort of Cool Hand Luke endeavor, Antarctica-style.

Michelle devised a method of carving small slices off the frozen brick, placing the pieces in individual Ziploc bags, and thawing each one as needed. Though its consistency was too homogenous and the color was much too yellow, the flavor did recall real eggs. Once cooked on a cast-iron pan over the small propane stovetop, omelets were delicious.

And, no, not once did I eat a real penguin egg. Wasn't even tempted. The skuas seemed to enjoy them.

Eggs, of course, aren't the only ingredients in an omelet. Frozen veggies, just like the ones in the frozen-foods aisle of the grocery store, were easy for us to thaw and mix in with the egg substitute. Corn, onions, and broccoli were nice, but a surplus of cauliflower

113

lasted until the end of the season. It tasted like soggy packing peanuts. Nobody likes frozen cauliflower.

We also hoarded a generous supply of frozen cheese to use on omelets. When thawed, this tasted just like fresh cheese, except it crumbled to the touch. The crumbly nature of frozen cheese made it difficult to slice, but otherwise cheese proved to be a favorite item for cooking and snacking. Several kinds were on ice, including cheddar and mozzarella.

Bricks of cheese were much easier to negotiate than the faux egg material. For one thing, the cheese was packaged in more manageable quantities. One brick would last a few days, a short enough period that, after thawing, it could be stored in the hut at room temperature, which varied from below freezing (at night) to forty or fifty degrees Fahrenheit (with the propane heater cranking during the day).

With cheesy omelets, bacon was a special treat. Luckily, uncooked bacon freezes well for long periods of time. We stocked up on lots of bacon at the beginning of the season, and rationed it as weeks went by. Bacon, I decided eventually, goes well with just about anything. Except maybe frozen cauliflower.

Omelets, though delicious, were an opportunistic meal whenever someone had the energy. Sundays were always pancake days. The first time I tried to cook flapjacks on the pan, I burned most of them. The unburned ones ripped in half when I flipped them, stuck to the pan, stuck to the spatula, or oozed uncooked batter from an inner magma chamber like mini Hawaiian volcanoes. I'm the kind of cook that requires directions—on a package of Kraft macaroni and cheese, I follow the steps faithfully—but eventually I figured out pancakes, to Michelle and Kirsten's amusement.

Toast was a little easier for me to manage. Frozen, sliced bread could be toasted on a special rack that rested directly on the stovetop. Peanut butter and jelly were also kept in our storeroom; it didn't matter if they froze once in a while. Pancakes and toast went together nicely.

114

My favorite breakfast, though, which I ate almost every day, involved several easy ingredients. It started with some dry oatmeal at the bottom of a large bowl. To this I added a layer of cereal, usually boxed granola. After sprinkling on a bit of soy milk powder, I used a ladle to pour ice-cold melted snow water in the bowl. Then I mixed everything. After the mixture soaked for a few minutes, I squeezed out a tablespoon of honey as garnish, and topped it off with two tablespoons of yogurt. Sometimes, as a treat, I added a few frozen raspberries or blueberries. Altogether, this was about as tasty as breakfast could get.

The yogurt was especially notable since fresh yogurt doesn't keep long, yet we ate fresh yogurt every day. It was more delicious than any yogurt in the store and we made it on the spot. A New Zealand company called EasiYo sells a clever yogurt maker that requires only boiling water, a powdered packet, and the EasiYo maker. This was perfect for our field camp. We filled a container with water, mixed in the packet, placed it in a special holder surrounded by boiling water, and, six hours later, perfect yogurt emerged. Like magic, every time. It was so good that I acquired my own EasiYo maker after I returned to civilization. I haven't bought yogurt since I went to Antarctica. Yogurtwise, the trip forever changed my life.

All of our food came from McMurdo Station and was dropped   115
with the rest of our gear at the beginning of the field season. One of the most interesting chores in McMurdo, before flying to Crozier, had involved packing the season's food.

Kirsten and I had taken the task of arranging all food supplies. We took our carefully filled-out grocery list to a special warehouse at McMurdo to collect the food. A very nice woman greeted us at the door, and accompanied us up and down the aisles to find the items we wanted. There was no question of price—all food for U.S. Antarctic Program research projects is provided by the National Science Foundation. Three months' worth of supplies was set aside and then packed securely into separate boxes, which, eventually, went to the Crozier hut.

Looking at the entire stack at McMurdo Station, visually dividing it into thirds, it was hard to imagine ever eating that much.

❋

Eternal sunshine encouraged longer cycles of sleep and activity. Time of day became irrelevant. Cave explorers, without reference to light, are known to relax from a twenty-four-hour schedule, and we were feeling the same effects in Antarctic sun. We slept later and stayed up later. Soon, Kirsten, Michelle, and I were waking up at eleven in the morning, heading into the penguin colony around four, and working outdoors until nearly midnight.

"If we sleep in and work one hour later each day, in twenty-four days we'll be back where we started!" I observed over dinner late one evening.

"But we'd lose a day in the process," commented Kirsten. "We need to stick with mechanized time." She was right. The only way to stay sane in twenty-four-hour sunshine was to follow the clocks. We began to set alarms to wake up and obeyed the demands of wristwatches. Still, our daily schedule was not your typical nine to five.

Soon after arriving at Crozier, I established a regular routine that seldom varied for the rest of my stay in Antarctica.

Typically, I woke to an alarm in my tent around 9:30. In biting cold, it usually took me half an hour to work up the courage to leave my sleeping bag, pull on snow boots, exit my tent, hit the outhouse, and slip inside the warm hut, all of which burned an additional fifteen minutes.

Michelle, Kirsten, and I sat down to breakfast at around 10:15. About eleven, I wiped down my breakfast plates with a paper towel (soap and water were too precious to waste on regular dishes). Then I hit the outhouse again. The importance of regular, well-formed bowel movements at a freezing camp cannot be overemphasized. Afterward, I flipped open my laptop. We spent the next hour sipping hot chocolate and entering data from

116

the previous afternoon. Mornings at Cape Crozier were quite civilized.

I went through my field notebook and carefully copied each resighted band number into a database program on my laptop, along with weather and condition information. The database gave instant histories about each bird so I could see where and when my penguins had been encountered over the years. Most birds returned to the same areas, but a few traveled between separate colonies on Ross Island, and we recorded some penguins from Beaufort Island, Cape Bird, and Cape Royds during our Crozier searches. For instance, at one point, out of 466 resighted penguins, fourteen were originally banded at other colonies. These were highlights of data entry.

We usually lunched around 12:30. I might eat a peanut butter and jelly sandwich, peanut butter and jelly bagel, peanut butter and jelly on toast, or random leftovers (like veggie burgers, without peanut butter and jelly) from the previous night's dinner.

At 1:15, we began to pack our daily gear for the field. Kirsten wrote a helpful checklist on a whiteboard inside the hut to make sure we didn't forget anything: databook, binoculars, radio, GPS, extra batteries, Sharpie, nest markers, Leatherman, water bottle, energy bars, goggles, extra changes of clothes, extra prescription glasses, sunglasses, satellite phone, handwarmers, sunscreen, and camera. It usually took fifteen minutes to pack.

Then we dressed for the field. I generally wore two pairs of long underwear, T-shirt, sweatshirt, fleece sweater, coverall pants, radio chest harness, heavy socks, gloves, hat, neck gaiter, sunglasses, heavy jacket and windbreaker, boots, and crampons— every time I left the hut. Extra clothing went into my backpack in case of emergency.

By 1:45, we were out the door. The one-mile downhill hike to the penguin colony was always a stroll compared to the return, uphill hike at the end of the day, and I usually felt glad to be outside in fresh air after spending the morning inside the stuffy hut. Waltzing down the glacier below our hut was a high point of my day.

117

By 2:30, I was among penguins. Unless another project was pressing, I wandered through sections of the colony looking for banded birds. I covered Area M most often, since marked birds were concentrated in that part of the valley, but also canvassed other areas. Kirsten, Michelle, and I were required to look at every single penguin—all quarter million of them—once every two weeks, to make sure no returning banded birds would be missed. Along the way, I gathered data for a few subprojects, including bagging eggshell samples for later lab analysis that might be useful for determining diet.

At 7:30, I turned my radio to the long-distance, McMurdo Station channel, to deliver a short, scripted check-in. "MacOps, MacOps, this is Bravo Zero-Three-One Cape Crozier on Mount Terror, how copy? Over."

"Loud and clear, Crozier. Continue, over."

"Three souls present and well at check-in. Any messages? Over."

"No messages today, Crozier. Anything else? Over."

"That's it. If nothing further, this is Bravo Zero-Three-One Cape Crozier, out."

"MacOps out."

The daily check-in was crucial. We were required to maintain at least two viable forms of communication with McMurdo Station at all times in case one broke down. If we missed a check-in, safety personnel would be dispatched immediately to begin a search, which would precipitate either an embarrassing situation or a life-saving mission. I heard several stories, tales, and Antarctic legends about people who missed their daily check-ins, whether by design or accident.

After the check-in, I scrambled up the face of Pat's Peak, a thousand-foot promontory overlooking the penguin colony. Its summit was higher than our hut and required a forty-five-minute hard climb from the valley floor. I spent an hour perched up there, scanning the ocean through a scope and binoculars to search for offshore whale activity. Scientists are interested in the whales because they might compete with penguins for food.

118

At 9:15, I dragged my cramped, cold muscles down the other side of the peak to reach the hut after a long day of field work. Michelle or Kirsten would have dinner going (unless it was my day to cook the meal, in which case I headed in early). We usually sat down to eat around 9:30. The hut was at its coziest in the evening, full of delicious steam, heat, and smells of food.

After dinner, we performed routine maintenance. This included straightening up the hut, tightening ropes on the tents outside, trouble-shooting the weather monitor, and other chores as needed.

At around 11:00, I propped open my laptop to check email. Satellite Internet was usually fast and reliable, and I never ceased to be amazed by the technology that had just been installed in the past couple years. These days, you can get Internet anywhere.

At midnight, I hit the outhouse one last time, and crawled through my frozen tent flap. Once inside, I shucked my snow boots, crawled into my sleeping bag, set an alarm for the next morning, and wriggled into a comfortable position. I never failed to lapse into deep, exhausted sleep.

24. Never Trust a Penguin

❄❄❄

"If we're going to visit the Emperor Penguin colony this season," said Michelle one morning, "we'd better do it soon. The sea ice is starting to break up."

Kirsten agreed immediately. "Yes, I've noticed," she said. "The edge of the ice is breaking in toward shore already."

A few hundred Emperor Penguins nest each year at Cape Crozier in a protected nook against the Ross Ice Shelf. I had watched them from the summit of Pat's Peak, using the spotting scope to get tantalizingly distant views, but the colony was several miles from our hut. To reach it, we'd have to cross several ice slopes, rock falls, boulder fields, and a large section of frozen ocean. The last part of the route lay directly across sea ice, which would soon drift away as a result of late-summer thawing temperatures, wind, and currents.

"Let's go tomorrow," Michelle suggested. "We should get a count of how many chicks are in the Emperor colony before it's too late."

In a moment, our new adventure was afoot. Assuming good weather, we planned to spend the next day hiking to the Emperor Penguins to count their chicks.

Over the rest of the day, I kept a constant watch on the skies from the Adélie valley while resighting banded birds, hoping desperately for the good weather to hold. Few people ever get the chance to see an Emperor Penguin, and even fewer see them nesting. To get close to such ancient, timeless birds is a once-in-a-lifetime experience.

Luckily, the next morning dawned bright, clear, and calm, and Kirsten, Michelle, and I set out early after breakfast for the long hike.

If you've ever seen *March of the Penguins* or *Happy Feet*,
you've seen Emperor Penguins. Along with Adélies, they are the
only penguin species restricted entirely to the Antarctic continent.
Unlike Adélies, though, Emperor Penguins lay their eggs in the
twenty-four-hour darkness and blinding blizzards of Antarctic
winter. The birds breed directly on sea ice, incubating their eggs
atop their feet instead of making nests. By the time spring comes
around, the Emperors already have large, fluffy chicks, almost
the size of adults. As the ice breaks out in late summer, the chicks
lose their fluffy coats, and both adults and fledglings swim out to
sea to spend the fall and early winter among pack ice. A normal
Emperor Penguin will never touch land in its entire life, which
may be up to fifty years long.

Since Charles Royds discovered the Crozier Emperor colony
on the Discovery Expedition in 1902, relatively few humans have
visited the spot. The penguins gather in a fractured nook against
the edge of the Ross Ice Shelf. This place is well chosen, protected
against the elements on three sides by thirty-foot-high walls of
sheltering glacial ice. Annual accumulations of guano, dead chick
carcasses, and eggshells are swept into the water when the sea
ice breaks in late summer and, by the time the Emperors return
in winter, the spot has refrozen and is perfectly clean, ready for
another nesting season.

Apsley Cherry-Garrard's journey included a visit to this exact
Emperor Penguin colony around 1910 as a side trip from Scott's
fatal South Pole expedition. Cherry, along with two others,
journeyed overland from the McMurdo Station area to Cape
Crozier expressly to collect Emperor Penguin eggs in mid-winter.
Though the trip was hellishly, heinously grueling, and nearly
ended the lives of all three explorers, the men eventually found
the Emperor Penguins, and became the first humans ever to see
them nesting.

A hundred years later, Michelle, Kirsten, and I followed in
Cherry's footsteps. From our hut, we first tacked inland, marching
uphill across a snowfield to skirt a rocky promontory called

121

Post Office Hill. The cliff faces on Post Office were full of deep nooks and caves that looked good for nesting Snow Petrels, and, as we hiked, we debated whether the delicate, snow-white birds were hidden high above. The discussion went unresolved, since those cliffs were mostly inaccessible. It would be very difficult to discover a Snow Petrel nest, though we'd often tried on nearby Pat's Peak, where the petrels occasionally dive-bombed our heads during sea watches, suggesting nesting behavior. Clambering on the cliffs, it was obvious why no Snow Petrels have ever been confirmed nesting on Ross Island, though the birds were a common daily sight during our field work.

Our route cut across the back side of Post Office Hill, transitioning from gentle snowfields to steep boulder slopes. We removed our crampons to walk over the crumbly, rocky surface, taking care not to twist an ankle on unstable terrain. I hopped nimbly from rock to rock, mindful of my forty-pound backpack.

The boulder field merged into another snowfield, which soon slanted uphill into an ice slope and a steep cornice. Crampons were essential here. Without the pointed metal spikes, our boots would not have been able to grasp the slippery surface, and it would be a long, terrifying slide to rocks far below. On one brief, exposed section, I felt momentarily like a Himalayan mountain climber. The ice was steep enough to touch the uphill side with my hand, smooth and hard as polished glass.

On the far side of the cornice, we topped out on an expansive rock-strewn area of bare dirt where a ridgeline flattened into a wide, table-like bench. A seasonal ice pool here had partially melted, and dozens of South Polar Skuas stood lined up at its edge, taking baths and drinking from the shallow, icy water.

Green smudges appeared nearby, at the edge of a snowfield. This, in Antarctica, passes for a forest. Green algae grew underneath the snow. The algae formed tiny mats less than one centimeter thick between rocks and snow, and these were a welcome sight, like an oasis in the desert.

Michelle, Kirsten, and I rested on the flat ridgetop, appreciating good views of the Ross Ice Shelf in the distance. We had been hiking for almost two hours.

"There goes a Snow Petrel," Michelle said, pointing above the coastline in front of us.

"Like a giant flying snowflake," Kirsten said.

The elegant, all-white bird knifed on the breeze, banking steeply from side to side to take advantage of small air currents. Like other petrels, it spends almost its entire life at sea, only returning to land to nest. This bird, unlike a penguin, is built for uninhibited flight. With long, tapered wings, the Snow Petrel barely needs to flap to maintain speed. It is one of very few birds in the world with entirely white plumage, the color of pure snow, set off by black eyes and feet.

"Do you think they might nest in ice caves?" Michelle wondered aloud. "I always see them soaring above that particular cornice."

"Not that I've ever heard of," I said. "I think they're just using wind currents on the cornice. All the Snow Petrel nesting references I could find described deep, narrow cracks and hollows in cliff faces and, occasionally, boulder fields. Not ice caves. Though I guess it's possible."

"Very few birds nest directly on ice," Kirsten said. "The only one I can think of in the world is the Emperor Penguin."

Our thoughts collectively turned to the Emperor colony waiting ahead.

"Let's motivate," Michelle said. "Not too much farther and we'll be there."

We donned our crampons to cross a long, gentle snowfield that slanted from Post Office Hill to the edge of the frozen Ross Sea. The last part of our route lay across the flat sea ice. The coastline was marked by a massive jumble of ice blocks and cracks. Though the ocean was frozen, tides and currents still affected the ice from underneath. Where land met sea, ice piled up in a chaotic collision zone, like a mini Himalayan range.

123

We pulled ice axes out of our backpacks and used them to probe the ice one step ahead as we edged on to the sea ice, hoping to discern thin spots before breaking through. Within the shoreline collision area, cracks continuously formed and refroze, and it was hard to tell where the thickest ice lay. Slabs and piles of ice were thrust twenty feet in the air in some places. Navigating through the jumble was like picking over a giant pile of demolished pavement chunks. The first hundred yards near shore was much more dangerous than the sea ice farther out. Here, potholes, cracks, and unstable formations criss-crossed the sea ice, and we used extreme caution while moving ahead.

Every so often, the sea ice shifted imperceptibly underfoot with unsettlingly loud, sudden cracks. Sometimes it sounded like gunfire, other times like a giant piece of metal sheeting being snapped in half. We weren't worried about it. The slow movements were driven by forces much greater than our own footsteps, but the noises were jarring and eerie.

Tides caused long cracks to form in the sea ice parallel to land near the shoreline. The cracks measured between an inch and two feet wide, and moved perceptibly, alternately widening and narrowing, with slushy seawater visible deep inside. Michelle, Kirsten, and I jumped over these cracks, making sure the far side would hold before we crossed.

124

While we picked our way through the ice jumble, Adélie Penguins crowded everywhere around, commuting between land and sea. They seemed to have just as much trouble crossing the rough terrain as we did. Unlike us, penguins couldn't easily step over large chunks of ice, and they were forced to find twisting, meandering paths through the maze. It was amusing to see one penguin climb a ten-foot-high mountain of ice before realizing it couldn't get back down; the bird agitatedly tried to tiptoe across a steep part, finally slipping, falling, and rolling all the way to the bottom. It popped quickly back to its feet, glanced around to see if anyone had noticed, and continued on its way.

The Adélies were full of energy, exploring new passages through the shoreline jumble. They were amazingly resilient, bouncing and ricocheting after clumsy slips and falls. Their toenails often kept the birds walking upright on outrageously slanted icy surfaces, but every penguin had its limits, and I appreciated watching their head-over-heels tumbles.

Experienced penguins followed established routes of least resistance through the ice maze, worn into grooved trails by thousands of tiny feet. Orderly lines of penguins walked single file, waddling one after another like roped mountain climbers.

I started to fall into line behind one such group of penguins, but Michelle stopped me short. "Wait—never trust a penguin!" she admonished.

"Huh?"

"Never trust a penguin," Michelle said again. "It bears repeating. They'll always lead you into trouble."

"That's right," Kirsten said. "Serious advice on ice navigation, actually."

Michelle explained further. "Look," she said, "you saw the penguin earlier fall off that hill? And the one that got itself trapped in a mini ice valley with no way out?"

"Yes," I said. "They were kind of funny."

"Penguins will walk anywhere," Michelle said. "They'll wander across the thinnest patches of ice, fall into open water holes, and swim through slushy spots. Occasionally, they get themselves into a real pickle. Somehow, penguins always end up on their feet, but the same can't be said for us. If we fell through a thin spot, we'd be in real trouble."

125

"Good point," I said.

"And," added Kirsten, "we're a lot heavier than an Adélie Penguin. Since they only weigh eight or ten pounds, those guys can get across seriously sketchy ice by flattening out their body mass and just skating across. No way would we be able to do the same thing."

"So," continued Michelle, "it's just bad news to tag along behind a penguin. He's not looking out for your best interests."

Kirsten smiled. "Even on established penguin trails over the ice, don't let yourself get careless. Those trails weren't meant to support humans. Stick with your own judgment about safe ice navigation."

"Got it," I said. "Never trust a penguin!"

We continued through the ice maze. Finally, Kirsten jumped over one last crack and spread her arms wide, embracing a limitless expanse of featureless, flat sea ice. "Welcome to the ocean!" she said. As far as the eye could see, the frozen sea surface lay unbroken. I stood on perfectly level, uniform hard-packed snow, coating several meters of solid ice. It was odd to think of the deep water underfoot.

An arm of the Ross Sea separated the Emperor colony from land by about a mile. We struck off across the sea ice toward the Ross Ice Shelf, boots crunching steadily closer to the Emperors.

Everywhere on the sea ice were Adélie Penguins. Some of them formed huge convoys, walking in lines and groups of tens or even hundreds. Others wobbled alone. A few penguins lay fast asleep as we passed. Others could be seen climbing the steep walls of the Ross Ice Shelf like miniature mountaineers.

As we approached the Emperor colony, hidden around a bend in the ice shelf, I kept my eyes out for anything larger than an Adélie. Knowing that an Emperor Penguin would reach my chest, I scanned the ice for tall silhouettes. When we were a quarter mile from the ice shelf, I spotted one.

126

"Check it out!" I said, pointing at a shadowy, slow-moving figure ahead. Michelle squinted into the distance, then turned with an expression of satisfaction. She confirmed the identification. "It's an Emperor Penguin!"

25. Gap Year

✳✳✳

I skipped my high school graduation party because I had to get up the next day at 4:30 a.m. to go birding. Fine with me.

By my great good luck, the American Birding Association, a twenty-thousand-member organization of like-minded bird folk, just happened to hold its annual convention in my hometown the very same week I graduated. In fact, the event was headquartered in a hotel lobby across the street from the graduation ceremony. After receiving my diploma, I ran outside, dodged a couple cars, and darted through the hotel's swinging doors to mix with an entirely different crowd.

Throughout middle and high school I'd been building a reputation as "that bird kid," spending thousands of hours wrapped in my obsession. I took every opportunity to let older birders drive me around, soaking up the experiences. When I obtained my driver's license, there was no looking back. I could finally find birds on my own.

Among non-birders, I kept my birding habits relatively quiet. None of my friends in high school was interested in birds, and many of them had no idea how I spent my time. Those who knew accepted my quirky addiction but didn't push the issue. For me, birding was a solitary, single-minded pursuit, more focused on birds than people. Tennis and other sports filled my social niches.

Priorities were about to change.

I planned to take a year off between high school and college. The concept was foreign to most of my friends, who were headed to university or—even worse, in my opinion—real jobs. Gap years are unusual in the U.S., though as many as one in eight students take them in Europe. During my year off, I was determined to focus full time on birding, and the ABA convention provided the kickoff.

While other graduates pulled an all-nighter, I set my alarm early. The dark hours before sunrise found me riding a chartered bus full of gray-haired tour participants toward dawn in the misty Cascade Mountains.

As an informed local birder, I was asked to help lead field trips during the convention. I had scouted locations ahead of time for woodpecker nests, warbler territories, and other "most-wanted" birds. Now that work paid off as I guided groups to the same spots, chatting up birders from all over the country, proudly wearing a yellow badge labeled "Trip Leader."

To my amazement, many of the attendees had heard of me. Even though I'd not done much birding outside of Oregon, they approached with extended hands, asking, "Are you that bird kid? I'm so glad to meet you!"

On the last evening of the convention, almost eight hundred birders crowded into a gigantic conference room for a banquet and entertainment. I'd never seen so many birders in my life, and only vaguely knew so many even existed. Most of them had flown in for the week-long event. Among the crowd were some of the most famous bird experts alive, and I was thrilled to rub shoulders with birding celebrities.

In a wrap-up during dinner, the keynote speaker paused before the banquet audience. "Now, I'd like to recognize some new talent," he said. "Noah Strycker, would you please stand up?"

Not knowing what to expect, I uncertainly pushed my seat back. People started applauding. Soon, everybody was cheering, and the whole place rose to its feet. Eight hundred birders sounded like sports fans in the tight room.

I was completely taken aback.

"Thank you," said the speaker, finally, and continued with his speech without further explanation. The birding community had shown their approval. It meant everything to me.

As a graduation gift, I received a week-long trip to Alaska with a group of Oregon birders. We spent several days in Nome, finish line of the famous Iditarod sled dog race, scrounging for ptarmigan (no luck) and Gyrfalcons (success!) in the long days

128

of Arctic summer, before flying to Saint Lawrence Island off
the coast of Siberia. This remote isle, within sight of Russia but
technically Alaskan, is the site of a small native village named
Gambell known for attracting stray Asian birds. Since it's the
closest American land to Siberia, Gambell is one of the best places
in U.S. territory to find Asian species.

Birding at Gambell was a bit surreal. Racks of reeking whale
blubber dried on the pebbled beach, obvious spoils of subsistence
hunting. Isolated vegetation grew in the fertile soils of several
boneyards—areas where natives had discarded animal scraps over
centuries of occupation—and these green oases attracted most of
the birds. I walked laps through the wet knee-high plants, kicking
aside scraps of ancient carved ivory artifacts, trying to flush odd
pipits and buntings, while the villagers roared past on their ATVs.
Rain and sleet stung on a sharp wind.

When a rare Little Bunting was discovered, I heard the
announcement on my FRS radio, a kind of walkie-talkie. Excited
about a species with fewer than ten U.S. records, I ran hastily
outdoors in my T-shirt, never mind the weather. I eventually saw
the unusual bird, but nearly froze to death in that godforsaken
boneyard.

The remote place appealed to my sense of adventure. As my
friends headed to college in the fall, I traveled instead to Malheur   129
National Wildlife Refuge to spend a season in the rugged high
desert of eastern Oregon. At refuge headquarters, I lived alone for
the first time in my life, thirty miles from the nearest settlement,
volunteered in the visitor center, ate beef with the ranchers, and
worked with refuge biologists during my four-month stay.

Near the end of the fall, my phone rang. It was Ted Floyd from
Colorado, the good-natured editor of *Birding* magazine, whom
I'd met for the first time at the ABA convention in Eugene. "Hey,
Noah, what do you think of an all-expenses-paid birding trip to
Taiwan?" he asked. "I've got an extra space."

I couldn't believe my ears. "I'm in," I replied, trying to keep
the excitement out of my voice. I could picture Ted's smile.

"We leave in nine days," he said. "I'll try to get your plane tickets booked right away. The Taiwanese government wants a small group of American and British birders to help design an ecotourism program. Basically, we'll be guided through the whole country for two weeks before giving feedback on the last day. I'll send full details with your tickets."

Nine days later, I was stalking the streets of Taipei. Our small group boasted a full-time birding guide, was chauffeured by a private driver, and stayed in four- and five-star hotels. We visited national parks, museums, botanical gardens, and reserves, edging toward the southern end of the country before hopping a train back north. I chopsticked every kind of seafood known to man, felt like a giant among the Taiwanese, learned a few Taiwanese words, didn't pay a cent, and, mostly, saw a ton of birds. Some of the Asian species for which I'd searched so hard in the freezing boneyards of Gambell were abundant in Taiwan, in the heart of their range, and I felt a little silly for having gone to such great lengths in the Arctic—but that's the game of birding.

Taiwan taught me a lesson about flexibility. Had I been enjoying a freshman year at college, I wouldn't have been able to leave at such short notice. Because of my gap year, I could vault off anywhere, anytime, to take advantage of any opportunity.

130   Of course, fortuity is seldom random. Ted had invited me on the trip after I'd written several articles for *Birding* and helped guide tours at the ABA convention. One thing led to another, and I was ready to step up where others couldn't.

After Taiwan, and a detour through Arizona to watch a professional tennis tournament, a couple weeks of birding in western Mexico, and two months of independent painting classes, I prepared for the culmination of my gap year.

Once again, an unpredictable chain of events led me to an unexpected place. Before high school graduation, I had decided to attend the University of Oregon. But somewhere between Alaska, Malheur, and Taiwan, an email came from Oregon State University professor and birder Douglas Robinson. His tone was friendly. He'd been paying attention to my local birding reports

and knew about some of my magazine articles. He invited me to
check out OSU's Fisheries and Wildlife program, second only to
Cornell University in number of bird-related faculty. Doug offered
to be my advisor and help with scholarships. Plus, he said, I could
work on his super-cool research project in Panama, regardless of
where I decided to go to college.

So, a few months later, I landed in Panama City for a four-
month internship with the Smithsonian Tropical Research
Institute to do field work for Doug's OSU project. I lived in
a beautiful house in Gamboa, alongside the central Panama
Canal, with another American and two Panamanians. The four
of us spent our days searching for bird nests in the suburban
yards of Gamboa and neighboring jungles, monitoring more
than seven hundred tropical bird nests over the course of the
season. On days off, I walked to Pipeline Road, accessing pristine
Soberanía National Park, one of the best birding destinations in
the American tropics—at least, when I wasn't hanging out with
National Geographic photographers, army ant scientists, and
local Panamanians.

The gap year proved to be an education and a blessing in every
way. I learned that flexibility has unforeseen benefits. I definitely
recommend everyone—yes, that means you!—to take a gap year
at some point. There is plenty of time to savor life before rushing
to the next step, and, like me, you may end up in places you never
imagined. Even returning to the same spot, you will have grown.

I also realized that I liked extremely remote destinations. What
if my gap year could be extended forever? Why would I ever need
a real job? With stipends and freelance work, I might be able to
pull it off. First, though, I needed to get a degree. After an action-
packed year of travel, I was ready to hit college.

OSU welcomed me with a full academic scholarship, and after
my gap year I began studies in the Fisheries and Wildlife program
fresh, focused, and eager. I would concentrate on academics and
tennis during the school year, and spend each summer doing
remote field work. It was a tidy arrangement, full of promise. I
couldn't wait for what lay ahead.

131

26. Emperors

❄❄❄

The Emperor moved slowly, deliberately, like a very old man without his cane. It was almost slothlike in energy, plodding along with shoulders hunched and a pinched, watery expression in the eyes.

This penguin was gorgeous. Unlike the impishly formal black-and-white Adélies, the adult Emperor showed off a splash of brilliant orange-yellow around its collar. Its head was pure black, soaking up black eyes, set off against a snowy-white front and black back with silver-frosted feather tips. The bird looked like a five-foot-tall bowling pin bent forward at the neck. Its long bill drooped at the tip, with a pinkish gape, giving it a slightly depressed expression.

What struck me most was the totally different aura this Emperor had. I was used to curious Adélies running circles around me, but this penguin couldn't have cared less. It walked methodically forward without any reaction to my presence. While Adélie Penguins were small kids bouncing off the walls, this Emperor was an aged, wise grandparent. It seemed to regard life as an endurance test, taken most easily one step at a time—literally.

Kirsten, Michelle, and I gave the penguin a wide berth. It appeared to be commuting from its colony on the ice to the open water several miles to seaward. Like Adélies, Emperor Penguins leave their chicks for multi-day feeding trips in the ocean, returning to regurgitate seafood to the waiting young penguins.

As we left the Emperor behind, we came across more adults on the sea ice ahead. The walls of the Ross Ice Shelf loomed tall just a few hundred yards away, massive and frozen in place. The Emperor Penguin colony was in a lead formed by a chink in the contour of the ice shelf, and, as we headed straight toward it, we passed several Emperors plodding steadily in the opposite direction.

Soon, the walls of the ice shelf began to close in on both sides as we worked our way inside the lead. Though the penguin colony wasn't visible, we knew it was just a few hundred yards ahead behind a bend.

A gigantic Weddell Seal lounged on the ice. Weddells are the most common of three seal species regularly encountered at Crozier (Weddell, Leopard, and Crabeater), and this animal was about twice my own length and at least ten times my girth. Intricately patterned with soft, muted gray and brown spotted designs on its fur, it looked exquisitely huggable, especially considering the floppy, broad flippers held close to its sides. With a teddy-bear expression in large, soft, round, faintly curious eyes, the seal smiled like the Cheshire cat beneath a set of bristling whiskers on each cheek. Its body was so blubbery that, as it stretched horizontally on the ice, the seal's head could barely touch ground.

Like the penguins, we walked a wide course around the Weddell, giving it the space and respect that Antarctica's wildlife deserves.

The lead narrowed, crossed a deep crack in the sea ice, and turned a sharp corner with the walls of the Ross Ice Shelf closing canyon-like on both sides. Just around the bend, I stopped mid-stride and sucked in an icy breath. "Whoa!"

"I'd say we're there," said Kirsten. All three of us ground to a halt.

Spread from one wall to the other and extending back into seeming infinity were hundreds of Emperor Penguins standing in dense groups. This first sight of the colony seared into my memory.

"Do you hear that?" asked Michelle. "Listen!"

A totally unexpected, chirping, high-pitched chorus greeted my ears. The Emperor Penguins' calls were understated, soft,

133

and relatively pleasant compared to the grating noises of Adélies. Sounds of begging chicks melded into one distinct audioscape that barely carried past the confined reaches of the colony.

Most of the crowd consisted of fluffy black-and-white chicks, interspersed with a few sleek and colorful adults. All the birds were standing, not moving much.

The Emperor Penguin chicks seemed to wear their grandmothers' Christmas sweaters. With downy feathers coating their plump bodies and tiny flippers, the young penguins were like kids overdressed for the cold. They also looked exactly like Mambo from the movie *Happy Feet*, with owlishly rounded, fluffy faces. In fact, since Emperor Penguins figure so prominently in popular media, the scene appeared like one big movie set.

Walls of the ice shelf rising sheer on one side, snow-covered mountains of Ross Island on the other, and alien-looking Emperor Penguins bunched all around created a prehistoric and timeless scene. Without my watch, I couldn't have been sure if we were in this millennium or the one before, or the one before that. Things haven't changed much for the Emperors in a long, long time.

"How many chicks do you think there are?" asked Michelle. Part of our duty was to census the colony.

"Hard to tell," Kirsten said. "Some of the penguins are far back in the lead, and I don't know if there might be more around the corner."

Michelle thought for a moment. "Let's take some photos, so we can count them later on a computer screen," she said. "And let's see if we can get a better vantage point of the whole colony."

Kirsten indicated the sheer wall of the ice shelf to one side. "We could climb up that," she suggested. "Might be a better view from up there."

It wasn't as crazy as it sounded. The ice was thirty or forty feet high, but, by using a ramp of drifted snow, we could scramble all the way up. The three of us carefully ascended the escarpment, careful not to punch through hidden mini-crevasses. When we reached the top, the whole Emperor colony spread out below us.

As a group, the Emperors seemed to move with their feet in molasses. Adults slowly shifted to and from the colony entrance, and the chicks didn't move much at all. But the place was full of life regardless.

Smaller Adélie Penguins ran around in loose groups, exploring among their much-larger relatives. The Adélies reached less than half the height of the bulky Emperors and exuded ten times the energy. I laughed when a group of Adélies swarmed around one slow-moving Emperor Penguin, parting like water around a rock. The Emperor stopped, blinked, and continued its plodding walk after the Adélies had passed.

I snapped a few photos, and Kirsten made an audio recording of the chicks' begging calls for later commentary. We also took a few images of the whole colony for later censusing with a GIS computer program.

The afternoon wore on, and the three of us turned for the long march home. We wouldn't reach the hut until midnight. With the sun always shining, we didn't worry about darkness on long field days like this.

"We'll have to see what the photos tell us, but I think there were around four hundred chicks," I said on the return trip.

"Sounds about right," Michelle replied. "We'll count them individually, of course."

135

"I just hope at least one sticks around until Christmas," I said, "which is a long time yet."

"Why?" asked Kirsten. "They should be done nesting and out to sea by then."

"So we can tally Emperor Penguin on our Christmas Bird Count," I said.

"What's that?" asked Michelle.

"We'll just have to see," I replied. And said no more about it.

27. Roughed Up

❋❋❋

"Hey, I noticed your bloody socks," Kirsten said to me just before dinner. "How are your feet doing?"

I'd clipped the socks in question over our propane heater to dry. They were standard-issue wool hiking socks that reached my upper calf. A round blood stain about an inch wide soaked each sock just above the heel.

I showed her the back of my foot.

"They match," I said. "Kind of a mess, actually."

After weeks of daily hiking on ice, my heels were blistered beyond recognition. The skin had bubbled, popped, and torn off so many times that ragged, bloody holes remained. During the day, they rubbed raw.

"Yikes!" Michelle said, leaning over to inspect the damage. "How can you walk?"

"With gritted teeth," I said, truthfully. "I don't think crampons agree with my feet."

"Do you need a couple days to rest?" asked Michelle. "You could just work on data for a while."

"No," I said. "It's fine. It'll heal eventually, and two days won't do much for blisters. I can hike, it's just uncomfortable."

No point in mentioning the times I had stopped, doubled over, and loudly cursed the ice, snow, rocks, boots, crampons, and life in general before limping along on my own. It's amazing how much pain one part of the heel can inflict.

In nearly two thousand miles of backpacking wilderness areas in the Pacific Northwest, I'd never suffered so much as a popped blister. In Antarctica, they were really breaking my stride.

"My latest experiment is with duct tape," I said. "I'm beginning to think it's more effective than blister strips, though the tape also peels off my skin after a while."

"You must have sweaty feet," Kirsten said.

"Yeah, I think these socks are pretty much sweated out," I admitted, unclipping one from the drying line to demonstrate. "See? It defies gravity!" Held sideways, the sock kept its shape, jutting out stiffly on a horizontal plane rather than drooping. Weeks of sweat and grime had imparted to it the consistency of cardboard.

"You might try washing them," Michelle said. "We do have some soap, though not much."

I grinned. "This is what it looks like after being cleaned," I explained. "I washed the socks last week. That's why there's not much soap left. Not that it did much good." I clipped the sock back in place and regarded it ruefully.

My blisters had started within days of beginning work at Crozier. Over weeks, they worsened to their current state. The hotspots were probably caused by crimping pressure from the crampon brackets above my heels, but there wasn't much to be done about it. Repeated efforts to tape, protect, and soothe the raw spots didn't make much difference. The blisters would have to sort themselves out.

All three of us were looking a little rough around the edges. My nose was peeling from the day I forgot to apply sunscreen, my lips were chapped, and my thumb was growing a huge hangnail. 137 Kirsten battled nosebleeds every so often, likely brought on by dry air, and Michelle was sore from hiking up the steep ice every afternoon.

We all fell regularly, sometimes landing hard. The ice was slippery, even while we were wearing crampon spikes, and its surface did not forgive a fall. One afternoon I wiped out on a particularly slippery spot, hitting the deck under my heavy pack, only to discover a body imprint in the snow nearby where Michelle had done exactly the same thing earlier. Glad not to have cracked a rib, I could only laugh.

Areas of loose rock were equally treacherous. After one fall amid a boulder slope on Pat's Peak, Kirsten warned me, "Don't break a leg! We're a long way from the hospital!" Neither of us could predict that, ironically, within a week of returning home from Antarctica, I would break my left leg while skiing over a precipice at Mount Bachelor, Oregon, necessitating surgery and two months on crutches—but that's another story.

While Kirsten started dinner, I dug out a mirror, curious to see my face. I had decided to give up shaving for the season. My cheeks were already covered in a matted blond beard. It added at least ten years to my appearance, especially combined with a ruddy, sunburned face, and grew thickly all the way down my neck.

"You look like the Mountain Man of the West," Michelle said. "About forty years old, I'd say."

"Do you think I look distinguished?" I asked.

Kirsten chortled. "How can anyone look distinguished with a dead animal on their face? Naw, you just look wild."

"You know, Thanksgiving is coming up," I said, changing the subject.

"No worries, we've got Cornish game hens covered," Kirsten said.

Michelle paused. "Thanksgiving isn't all about food," she said. "It's family we're really going to miss this year."

"Well, we can try to make up for it with the meal," I suggested.

I tried not to think about turkey, ham, sausages, cranberry sauce, apples, green beans, mashed potatoes, gravy, casseroles, fresh salad, squash, corn on the cob, cornbread, fresh milk, cider, pumpkin pie, and blackberry cobbler. But images of rich foods kept running through my mind. Thanksgiving dinner in Antarctica could never live up to a traditional American blowout. Or could it?

28. Blondie and Blackie

✳✳✳

Blondie and I met on a chilly, overcast morning, with the wind blowing from the south and a lenticular cloud settling menacingly over Mount Terror. That extra edge in the air gave our introduction special salience, but he was the type to stand out anyway.

Michelle and Kirsten had already told me Blondie's story over breakfast.

"You can spot him a mile away," Michelle said, nursing a cup of hot chocolate. "Literally. He's like a piece of milk chocolate among chocolate chips."

"Or a Fruit Loop in a bowl of Cheerios," Kirsten added, stirring her cereal.

"What makes him stick out?" I asked. "All the penguins look alike."

"Except for Blondie," Michelle said. After a pause, she explained. "Blondie is a male penguin who looks a bit different from the rest. Instead of having a black back, flippers, head, and tail, he's startlingly blond. Hence the name."

"It's a natural issue with the melanin pigments in his plumage," Kirsten said. "Not enough pigment is present to produce the glossy black of normal penguins, so the feathers grow out blond. Kind of like an albino, except not quite as extreme."

"So," I clarified, "Blondie is a penguin that doesn't fit in."

"Right," Michelle said.

It would certainly be easy to pick out a blond penguin among the masses of black ones. The bird would have no place to hide.

This got me wondering. Do penguins discriminate based on color? Females are known to choose their mates according to fitness, but would color have anything to do with it?

139

"How's his social life?" I asked. "Do the other penguins make fun of him?"

"Well," Kirsten said, "Blondie has one of the best territories in the entire Crozier colony. His nest is on top of a small hill in Area L, right next to the ocean, so he has a great view and a short commute to sea. He seems as healthy as a penguin could be."

"Sounds like a pretty good life for a penguin," I said. "Maybe he's independently wealthy."

Michelle looked amused. "Yes," she said, "he seems happy, except for one thing. He's never found a girl. Blondie has returned faithfully to defend the same nest at least seven summers in a row, but he always spends the entire season alone. He's never had a mate. Whether or not that relates to his odd coloration is debatable, but most adult male penguins—especially with such a good territory—seem to hook up with a female sooner or later. Blondie, much as we love him, has been ignored by girl penguins."

The story struck me as unaccountably sad in human context, but perhaps not for a penguin. Maybe Blondie was an optimist. At least, that would explain why he returned year after year to sit alone on the same rock.

Anthropomorphic comparisons aside, there just wasn't much else for Blondie to do. He was a penguin, and penguins made nests. Even an odd-looking one had to follow the plan. Who knew what thoughts ricocheted behind his beak.

"He's back this year, by the way," cut in Kirsten. "I saw him at his usual nest the other day. You should check him out—Blondie is a beautiful bird." She grabbed a laminated aerial photo map and pointed out the location. "He could be out on a feeding trip," Kirsten said, "but he'll defend his nest all season, now. We'll just have to watch how things go for him as the season progresses."

Later that morning, after the three of us had packed, hiked to the colony, and split up to canvass banded penguins, I paid a visit to Blondie's nest.

It was a cold, breezy day to be studying penguins. An unusual, thin veil of overcast blotted out the sun, throwing the snow and ice into a flat, two-dimensional perspective. The sky appeared the same color as the ice. A lenticular cloud formed at the summit of Mount Terror, a sure sign of windy weather ahead.

Blondie was right where he was supposed to be. He lay at ease on his nest in a half state of consciousness, just like all the other neighboring penguins. With feathers the color of honey and brown sugar, he was easy to pick out from the crowd. The blond plumage looked very soft, and I fought the sudden urge to walk up and pet Blondie's back. Perhaps the light color accentuated the layers of fine, bristle-like feathers, which usually blend together in a solid sheet of black.

"How you doing, huh?" I whispered. "Back for another summer, hoping to get lucky this time?"

Blondie was alone at his nest, but that didn't mean he lacked a mate. At this time of the season, most penguins were incubating eggs, and, while one sat on the nest, its partner foraged at sea. An egg would be the best clue that Blondie had unexpectedly found a girl. If there was no egg, he probably remained a bachelor, since paired penguins usually hung out together until the eggs were laid.

I had to see if Blondie was sitting on an egg or an empty nest. Rather than disturb him, I sat down on a frozen rock to wait for him to shift positions.

141

With inactivity, the cold sank in, and I was soon forced to bounce around on my seat to generate heat. But Blondie just sprawled unmoving on his nest except for an occasional flicker of the eyelid. The longer he didn't move, the more likely it was that no egg lay underneath, since incubating penguins obsessively stand up to realign their eggs. But I wanted to be sure.

Eventually, fate intervened. A wandering penguin waddled too close to Blondie's nest, and he stood up, lashing out with a vicious volley of pecks to move the intruder away. The defense seemed more hasty and aggressive than usual, and I quickly saw a reason for his bad temper. The nest, a neat cup of pebbles, sat empty.

Once again, Blondie was alone at the party.

❋

Blondie wasn't the only weird-looking character at Crozier. Among the quarter-million penguins, I saw more than half a dozen aberrant birds with odd plumages.

Several, like Blondie, lacked enough melanin pigments to turn their feathers black. This deficiency expressed itself to different degrees, and a few penguins appeared with various light shades approaching Blondie's extreme golden color. One bird, which we nicknamed "The Strawberry Blond," sported distinctive reddish-brown hues as if it had been highlighted at a styling parlor.

At least two other adult penguins were partially albino, showing white areas where normal Adélies were colored black. One individual, dubbed the "Ghost Penguin" by Michelle after she spotted it wandering waif-like through the colony, was almost completely white except for a gray wash over parts of its back. Another penguin turned up with checkered black and white patterns on its back, white flippers and tail, and a bright red beak. We named this one the "Tropicbird Penguin" for a wild resemblance to another, totally unrelated seabird called the Red-billed Tropicbird.

Fully albino, all-white penguins are generally rarer and, of the albinos that do occur, few survive past the nestling stage. I saw one albino chick at Crozier, with bubblegum-pink skin and wispy, snowy-white downy feathers (contrasted with the normal, dark gray chicks around it), but it disappeared within days of hatching. Since its white plumage stuck out, the unlucky chick presented a clear target for marauding skuas and was quickly eaten.

The most interesting variants were the penguins with too much black coloration. Over the season, I saw three adult penguins with black feathers in normally white spots. One, which I called the "Superhero Penguin," looked just like a normal Adélie with an extra armored chest plate. Instead of being confined to the throat, black color extended most of the way down its belly, ending in a ragged black and white border. The Superhero lived in the East Colony, which required a long trek, so we didn't visit him often.

Even more interesting was an almost entirely black male penguin in Area H. Except for a few whitish smudges on his lower belly and flanks, the bird could have been dipped in ink. He seemed to have applied blackface to hide the usual conspicuous white underparts. Like Blondie, he couldn't seem to attract a girl, but never gave up industrious efforts to build the biggest nest in his subcolony. By the end of the season, the black penguin defended a veritable fortress of loose stones, piled several inches high and two feet wide, mostly stolen from neighboring "normal" birds.

Most beautiful of all, though, was a female we called "Blackie." Blackie and I got acquainted one morning after an unusual snowstorm dumped several inches of powder throughout the penguin colony overnight. Kirsten guided me on a special visit to the bird, which had returned to the same nest several years in a row.

Crozier looked completely different under its fluffy white blanket of snow. Usually, wind kept many rocky areas clear, but this morning was calm, and snow had accumulated in thick powdery layers. The penguins stayed on their nests throughout the snowstorm, and their body heat melted small patches of bare ground surrounding each nest. The incubating birds, evenly spaced, looked like ants on spilled sugar.

143

Kirsten and I crunched our way between long, swirling subcolonies of penguins, leaving meandering twin trails of boot tracks in the snow to mark our passage.

"So, Blackie is, uh, all black?" I asked.

"Yep," Kirsten said. "She's the most glamorous penguin in the colony."

"She?" I clarified. "It's a she?"

"Definitely," Kirsten said. "Wait until you see her mate. No question."

Structure is the best way to differentiate between male and female Adélie Penguins in the field, but sometimes this can be hard to judge. Males tend to have larger bodies, with blockier heads and thicker beaks. When a male and female stand next to each other, the close comparison is especially helpful.

We trudged around a headland and over a ridge, finally descending into the parallel valley identified as Area T on my aerial photo map. Along the floor of this valley, a perennial strip of snow and ice funneled commuting penguins from upper slopes to the sea, and the lower end of this strip was loaded with heavy two-way traffic. This was the "Penguin Superhighway," delivering penguins to their destination with the efficiency of a four-lane interstate.

Kirsten took us to the shoulder of the Superhighway and abruptly set down her pack in the snow. She slid open the cinch and grabbed her camera, securely packed among extra layers of clothing inside the pouch. When she saw me gazing aimlessly at the tide of commuting penguins, Kirsten smiled. "No, don't look at the Superhighway," she instructed. "Over there—that's Blackie!"

With her camera, she gestured at right angles toward a small, isolated subcolony of penguin nests in a tight group alongside the Superhighway. At the edge of the group, one penguin stood out from its neighbors. On closer inspection, it appeared to be entirely black except for the usual reddish beak and wide, staring eyes. Every feather was perfectly and uniformly dark.

144

"Wow!" I exclaimed. "She's blacked out, all right."

Blackie sat on her nest in the typical prone position of incubating penguins. Even in this pose, it was obvious she had completely black breast, belly, and flanks. Surrounded by fresh, white snow, Blackie seemed to soak up all color in a black hole above her nest.

"She's got at least one egg," Kirsten said. "I saw her adjust it a few days ago."

"So, Blackie's got a mate," I mused, "unlike Blondie, who never seems to attract that kind of attention. I wonder if girl penguins gain an advantage with odd plumages."

"You must admit she's beautiful," said Kirsten, admiringly.

"She's gorgeous," I replied.

Blackie was definitely the sleekest, sexiest penguin I'd seen. Her variant black plumage was nearly iridescent with a glossy sheen. When she puffed her feathers to stay warm while incubating, the shadows between the feather tips created a deep, three-dimensional aspect of dark hues. The bird's look embodied an essence of cool, midnight style, like a black jaguar on a grand piano. Rather than sitting stiffly on her nest, Blackie lounged there as if on a bar stool. She fixed us with an unconcerned, penetrating stare, indifferent to our conversation.

I stared, but Kirsten was looking around as she snapped photos. "There's Blackie's mate," she said. "Standing right behind her. Geez, that's the biggest Adélie Penguin I've ever seen."

Sure enough, an enormous normal-colored male Adélie towered protectively over Blackie's left flank. Like humans, individual penguins vary in size, and this one must have been the equivalent of a star football linebacker.

"So, she's quite a catch," I said. "Blackie landed the best mate in the colony."

He stood perfectly straight and alert in the snow, likewise unconcerned about us, but keeping a constant eye out for aggressive skuas or other dangers. Something in the way this individual penguin was built suggested latent power. He had a massively thick beak for an Adélie, his head was blocky like a brick, and passing penguins steered well clear as he guarded Blackie and her nest like a bouncer. Unless I was mistaken, Linebacker treated Blackie as a trophy.

How different were the love stories of Blondie and Blackie, I mused, though they both maintained good territories. Blondie, alone, had faced seven years of bad luck. Blackie, however, seemed to gain social status by her sleek, unusual plumage, and was happily involved with an alpha male penguin. What might have happened if Blondie and Blackie had been introduced at the right moment? The two penguins had probably never even seen each other. They lived on different sides of the Crozier metropolis, each caught in its own story.

145

Blondie's life, though, would soon take an unexpected turn.

✳

A couple weeks later, Kirsten burst into the hut after a long day of work in the colony, still out of breath from the hard climb up the glacier. "Hey!" she panted, slouching in one of the metal chairs to catch wind. "You'll never believe it!"

Michelle paused with a pan in one hand, in the midst of preparing pitas with chicken and yogurt sauce for dinner. I sat in my usual seat with my back to the propane heater, entering band sightings on a laptop. "What?" Michelle and I asked at once.

"You'll never believe it," Kirsten repeated. "It's incredible. Totally unexpected. I've got the best news!"

"What?" we asked again.

"Guys, people, world headlines," said Kirsten. "Wait for it ..."

"WHAT?"

"Blondie's got an egg!"

"No way," said Michelle. She put down her pan and scratched her head.

"No way!" I whooped. "That means Blondie found a girl!"

"Yep," Kirsten said. "He couldn't have laid it himself. He got himself a woman."

After seven years of bad luck, Blondie had broken his loneliness. Questions flooded to mind all at once.

"What's she look like?" I asked.

"Was Blondie sitting on the egg, or was it the girl?" Michelle asked.

"One or two eggs?"

"Is she, uh, normal?"

Kirsten smiled as she regained her breath. "One at a time, please," she said, putting up a dismissive hand. "First things first."

Michelle and I sat in expectant silence for Kirsten's story. "I was down around Area L," she said, "and figured I'd check on Blondie as I passed, just to make sure he was still kicking. I could see his blond hide sticking out from a mile away, as usual, but, for some reason, decided to pay a closer visit."

She shifted in her chair. "When I got up close I could tell that he was standing upright, fiddling with something in his nest. Turned out, it was an egg! Just one egg, not two. He was very tender, and did a great job incubating while I watched, like he'd been nesting for years. Blondie's a natural family man." Kirsten winked.

"But," I cut in, "what does the girl look like? Is she, you know, like the other penguins?"

Kirsten frowned. "I didn't see her," she said. "She must have been out on a feeding trip."

"I want to see who broke Blondie's bad streak!" said Michelle.

"Go down there and look for yourself," Kirsten said. "But rest assured Blondie's having a good year."

For almost two weeks, Blondie's mate remained cloaked in mystery. Every time one of us checked, Blondie was alone, happily incubating his egg. But he couldn't have laid it himself. Short of a random female dumping an egg in his nest (which was possible; I knew of one or two penguin nests with three eggs, which suggested egg dumping happened at least occasionally), he must have been waiting for his girl to return from a long feeding trip.

One afternoon, beginning to give up hope, I swung by Blondie's nest. As I arrived at Area L, I thought I must have taken a wrong turn. Blondie was nowhere to be seen. The entire subcolony was filled with normal-looking penguins.

147

I traced my way to Blondie's exact nest, and the mystery was solved. In Blondie's place, there was a healthy, normal-looking girl penguin, contentedly incubating his egg while he took a break at sea. Without Blondie, the nest no longer stuck out. Blondie's girl kept her egg warm just like hundreds of thousands of other penguins.

In the end, both Blondie and Blackie raised normal-looking baby penguins. Their odd plumage discolorations must have been due to recessive genes. The "normal" adults that mated with Blondie and Blackie rewarded their mates with perfectly healthy penguin families. When they disappeared at the end of the summer, I hoped that Blondie and Blackie would return for another year in the colony. First, though, they'd have to make it through the long winter ahead.

29. Seawatching

✳✳✳

Barely visible on the horizon, a fin splashed in the sunlight. Two black, rounded shapes broke the sea surface, and fine spray spouted like a distant garden mister. My spotting scope was focused on the action, and I zoomed for a closer look with the high-powered optics. Movement flashed on glassy, calm water more than a mile away. With the sun at my back, the lighting was ideal.

Finer details were visible through the scope. A pod of Orcas (Killer Whales) traveled along the edge of the Ross Ice Shelf. Their sleek dorsal fins, long and narrow, cut the water sharply as each individual surfaced for air. Males could be identified by longer, larger fins, sticking up like enormous black rapiers, marking an aggressive and lurking presence below.

I pulled out my field notebook and penciled a few observations.

"Looks like at least a dozen of them," I muttered, squinting against a chilly breeze. It was very hard to count the number of Orcas in the group. Individuals constantly surfaced and submerged, and I tried to keep track of how many could be discerned simultaneously. I talked myself through an estimate. "Probably about fifteen," I said to the breeze. "Heading parallel to the ice shelf."

The sea ice broke out in a short blizzard just before Thanksgiving. Less than a day after our march to the Emperor Penguin colony, overnight winds blew the fractured pieces away from shore, leaving a wide area of deep blue, shimmering water and a band of jumbled pack ice. For the first time, open water cut the icy view of the Ross Sea, gently heaving with slow summer swells.

We were lucky. Gone was the mile-long section of ice we'd waltzed across. If Michelle, Kirsten, and I had waited one more day, the Emperors would have been inaccessible behind an arm of unfrozen sea.

Orcas and gray, small-finned Minke Whales arrived soon afterward. They used the patch of open water as a staging area for feeding trips underneath the edge of the ice shelf, taking advantage of high concentrations of krill, cod, and other marine life. Where we had hiked over solid ice to the Emperor Penguin colony, whales now splashed and spouted, enjoying the freed area.

With the influx of interesting mega-wildlife, Michelle, Kirsten, and I began to split time on new seawatching duties. Every day, one of us scrambled to the top of Pat's Peak between our hut and the penguin colony and spent an hour glassing the distant ocean for whales. We stashed a spotting scope among the rocks at the summit next to a natural bench. Getting up there required a tough twenty-minute climb over unsteady rocks and ice. Sweat dripped off my nose by the time I topped out, but the perspiration quickly froze in place after I settled into quiet vigil.

Scientists are interested in whale activity at Cape Crozier because the Orcas and Minkes, which arrive mid-season when the ice cover dissipates, eat many of the same things as penguins. As the season progresses, penguins must forage farther and deeper to find enough food. Presumably, local marine life is depleted by a quarter-million penguins concentrating in such a small area. This is one reason why penguin colonies don't get much bigger. But researchers have recently observed that whales might further deplete marine prey near the penguin colony, affecting penguin feeding habits. Our whale observations would be compared with penguin behavior data to determine what indirect interactions might be at work.

From my perch on the peak's rocky summit, the view was terrific. The Ross Ice Shelf extended to the horizon in one direction, dramatically dropping into the Ross Sea, while Mount Terror loomed inland.

The group of Orcas moved steadily along for a few minutes. I could make out the distinctive white teardrop patches above and behind their eyes when each one surfaced. As with most Killer Whales observed at Crozier, the white patch slanted aggressively forward on these individuals, indicating they belonged to the "Type C" variety—restricted to Antarctic waters, observed by few humans, rarely photographed, not known to prey on penguins, and likely to represent an entirely unrecognized species of Orca.

According to procedure, I noted the time, location, and duration of surfacing in my field notebook. I'd mastered the technique of flipping its thin pages with gloved hands since bare fingers would have quickly numbed in the cold.

When the Killer Whales disappeared into chilly depths beneath the ice, I returned to purposeful horizon scans through the scope from my high perch. Every so often, a fairy-like Snow Petrel wafted through my field of view, but no other whales broke the surface. From this elevated perspective, swimming Adélie Penguins appeared as tiny dark specks while they porpoised through the water. The penguins enjoyed close access to the sea, and large groups lined up at the ice edge, waiting for their chance to dive in.

Even with thick gloves, stiffness crept into my fingers while I operated the scope. Its metal housing seemed to absorb my heat. The hour-long, stationary seawatch ended with cold and cramped muscles, despite layers of clothes and a tummyful of hot chocolate.

151

When time was up, I stashed the scope, tethering it securely to frozen rocks, and shouldered my pack for a descent down the back ridge of Pat's Peak. The sketchy summit pitch required a controlled slide through an exposed scree slope followed by a long snowfield steep enough to require kicking individual steps. A slip in the wrong place could result in a nasty fall.

Time for another day at work in the penguin colony. Distant whales entertained, but they could never compare with the endless fascination of close-up penguins. I hummed to myself while carefully picking through the rocks. As I descended into the valley, the sounds and smells of penguins gradually amplified. I squinted into the clear sky, thankful for the bright sunshine.

My peripheral vision caught an anomaly in the heavens. Something unusual floated against the azure expanse.

I paused, balancing on the steep snowfield to crane skyward. As my sight focused, I gaped in disbelief. High above the Antarctic continent, a round, shimmering, unnatural, metallic object hovered in defiance of gravity.

"Michelle!" I thumbed the transmit button on my VHF radio, clipped in its chest harness. "Can you hear me? Kirsten?"

A scratchy reply came through. "Yes?"

I hesitated briefly, not sure what to say.

"Do you see it?" I asked. "There's a UFO above the penguin colony!"

30. Satellite Tags

❄❄❄

"It's not a UFO," Michelle said over the radio. "It's one of those giant scientific balloons launched from McMurdo Station."

From my spot on the back side of Pat's Peak, I watched the round, shimmering object hovering high above the continent. "But what if it is an Unidentified Flying Object?" I argued. "How can you be sure?"

Kirsten joined the radio conversation. "Then we're all at the mercy of the aliens," she said. "But, trust me, it's a well-known project."

As it turned out, Michelle and Kirsten were right. The mysterious craft was in fact a gigantic inflated sack carrying a payload of high-tech equipment in Earth's upper atmosphere. It was one of three released from McMurdo, forty-five miles away, over the course of the season.

Though not a UFO, the balloon recalled science fiction. It floated at an altitude of one hundred and thirty thousand feet (about twenty-five vertical miles) over Antarctica, dangling a payload of instruments able to monitor antimatter and cosmic rays—some of the most elusive elements in space. A $270 million monitoring station under construction at the South Pole would measure related neutrino particles. With these types of observations, scientists hoped to draw new conclusions about the construction of the universe.

David, my roommate during my first week at McMurdo Station, had been involved in the balloon project. I remembered his ready smile as he nicknamed me "Bird Man of Antarctica," and wondered what the guy was up to.

Meanwhile, we prepared to deploy our own cutting-edge technology on the backs of penguins at Cape Crozier. The PenguinScience project had stocked us with five precious satellite

153

tags for use on adult birds. Tags taped to individual penguins would continuously upload GPS coordinates, pressure, light, and temperature data to satellites, which would bounce that information straight to email. In theory, we would be able to sit inside the Antarctic hut and watch our penguins go out to sea, all on the screen of a laptop.

But first someone had to wrangle a few penguins.

Ideally, the satellite tags would be deployed on birds with medium-sized chicks to take advantage of one- or two-day oceanic feeding trips. We could then retrieve the tags fast enough to rotate them to other adult penguins. We were ready to start tracking. Whenever chicks began to hatch.

On a chilly morning in early December, I spotted my first penguin chick. Its sound attracted my attention. I heard an odd, weak, high-pitched, begging call, and tracked the noise to its source, delighted to discover a tiny, fuzzy head poking from underneath its parent's belly.

Within a week, the entire colony was transformed by penguin chicks hatching all over the place. Their thin voices mixed with the guttural sounds of adults. Where thousands of penguins had been calmly sitting on eggs, birds now bustled and fussily tended babies.

"It's the beginning of chaos," Michelle said grimly. "Just wait. Things are going to get messy."

Pretty soon, many chicks had reached the right age for us to track their parents by satellite. Michelle, Kirsten, and I dusted off the tags, each about the size of a Snickers bar with a four-inch antenna, and headed into the colony one morning to find some suitable penguins.

Michelle instructed me on the finer points of penguin wrangling. "Watch first," she said, gesturing as Kirsten advanced on a targeted bird. "Most of the time, all you have to do to catch a penguin is walk over and pick it up. But sometimes they get a little cagey. The idea is to grab the feet with your left hand and the base of the tail with your right hand, then sweep the penguin into your armpit. Don't hesitate, or the penguin will try to run away. Just go for it."

Kirsten knelt down next to the penguin at its nest, pretended to focus on a neighboring bird, and suddenly pounced. In a matter of seconds, she had subdued the struggling penguin in her arms, and held it tightly in place. "See?" Kirsten demonstrated, squatting on a patch of bare rocks with the penguin in her lap. "With a firm hold on it, I can safely handle this bird with one hand. I have total control without hurting it."

We quickly secured a satellite tag in a streamlined position to the center of the penguin's back, using special water-resistant tape to affix it against the bristle-like feathers. We also attached a small radio telemetry transmitter so the bird could be tracked manually with antenna and headphones. Once released, the penguin waddled back to the chicks in its nest, none the worse for its momentary abduction.

"Your turn," Kirsten said. "Let's find one for you to wrangle."

After some searching, Michelle found another adult penguin with chicks of the right age. "Over here!" she waved. "Got one for you!"

I sized up my quarry. I figured I could handle a two-foot-tall, ten-pound bird, even one with strong flippers and a sharp beak. The penguin, not to be intimidated, affixed me with a curious stare.

As I advanced, though, the penguin retreated. I walked faster, and the wily animal darted behind a neighbor's nest, staying just out of reach. Soon, I was chasing it in circles, getting nowhere, while we tired each other out.

"Let's find another one for you," Michelle said at last. "You lost the element of surprise with that penguin. Remember, be quick and confident—don't hesitate."

My second attempt went more smoothly. As I approached the next penguin, it settled in defense over its nest. I quickly reached down and grabbed the bird's legs, then, having gained the upper

155

hand, so to speak, lifted it against my chest and armpit. Once the penguin was secure, I dropped a warm hat over its unguarded chicks inside the nest to prevent them from running away or being attacked by a skua. The soft, wriggling hat brought a smile.

As I held the penguin, Michelle and Kirsten efficiently attached a satellite transmitter to its back. "Have a good journey," Kirsten said, affectionately, as the bird was released a minute later. We stood back to watch it instinctively return to its nest and chicks. If all went well, the penguin's mate would return soon from a feeding trip in the ocean. The pair would switch duties at the nest, and our tagged bird would head to sea alone for a couple days. When it returned, we'd be ready to retrieve its expensive tag.

Unfortunately, this one would decide to return at 4:30 a.m. And it would be up to me to wrangle it, alone on the ice.

31. Thanksgiving

✳✳✳

"Happy Turkey Day!" I beamed to Kirsten and Michelle as we huddled next to a large subcolony of penguins.

"Yeah, I almost forgot," Kirsten said. "Turkeys are kind of a foreign concept."

"Me, too," admitted Michelle.

"It's hard to remember the holidays when they don't mean much," I agreed.

On Thanksgiving Day, we were in the midst of a censusing project. Two days before, a helicopter had flown over the colony to take aerial photos. Eventually, some poor soul in a university office would painstakingly count every single speck on those images, each dot representing a penguin, to get an accurate population estimate—somewhere around three hundred thousand birds. Still, the photographs were just a good index. To ground-truth the aerial census, our Crozier crew performed actual counts of selected subcolonies.

So on Thanksgiving Day Kirsten, Michelle, and I worked our way around the valley together, clutching handheld mechanical counters while visually sifting through thousands of penguins. After finishing each subcolony, we compared our totals. If the numbers were too different, we counted twice.

"I got one thousand, four hundred and thirty-seven penguins for that one," I said.

Michelle wrote the number in her field notebook and turned expectantly to Kirsten. "One thousand, three hundred and eighty-nine," she said, evenly.

"Dang," Michelle replied. "I got one thousand, three hundred and twelve. Too far off. We'll have to count this one again."

We spread out in resignation along the edge of the subcolony, reset our counters to zero, and began afresh. I started at one end of the meandering concentration of penguin nests, letting my eyes flick quickly from one bird to the next. It was easiest to construct abstract shapes inside large groups, running visually along mental rows. For each additional penguin, my thumb hit the counter trigger, turning over a new digit.

It was good to be outside. The previous twenty-four hours had been stressful, busy, and cramped. Three techs had been flown from McMurdo Station to fix our satellite Internet and electrical systems the preceding afternoon. They succeeded, but, by the time things were working again, weather had clamped an icy fist over Crozier. Fifty-mile-per-hour winds whipped up a partial whiteout, preventing the helicopter from retrieving our visitors. In an anxious moment, the helo pilot hovered his craft outside our hut's window, buffeted sideways by wind gusts, while apologizing to us over the radio. "I can't shoot the approach, guys," he said. "I'm heading back to station." With that, the machine turned, lifted, and disappeared behind a curtain of rotor-driven snow, beginning a solitary forty-five-mile retreat to McMurdo.

The three guys hadn't expected to be trapped at our field camp on Thanksgiving Eve and had brought only enough supplies for a day trip. In our enforced captivity, I cooked everyone dinner and played music on a laptop while Kirsten and Michelle tidied up to accommodate our guests. We fitted them with emergency sleeping bags, but the hut was cramped with six people, and there weren't enough bunks to go around, since Michelle, Kirsten, and I were also forced to sleep indoors. Two good-natured communications techs slept on the narrow floor.

The blizzard, though strong enough to pin us indoors, wasn't a big one, and blew itself out overnight. On Thanksgiving morning, fitful gusts tickled our camp, but a helicopter could settle long enough to evacuate the McMurdo guys, who were relieved to leave in time for a real dinner at the American station. Kirsten, Michelle, and I waved goodbye as the mechanical bird twirled away, and admired a special holiday present delivered by its pilot: one semi-fresh onion wrapped in a brown paper bag. We suited up for our ground counts in the penguin colony, happy to be alone again.

On the second pass, our totals aligned much better.

"One thousand, four hundred and two," I said, counter in hand.

"One thousand, three hundred and eighty-four," said Kirsten.

"Great!" breathed Michelle. "I got one thousand, three hundred and ninety-six. That's as good as it gets."

We moved on to the next target, using a map to navigate to specific subcolonies. After several hours, we had each counted nearly ten thousand individual penguins, many of them multiple times, providing a solid baseline for the aerial census. The three of us split up for the rest of the afternoon to search for banded penguins. Kirsten packed it in early, as was customary for whoever cooked dinner.

Meanwhile, covering my daily route through the penguin colony, I made an unusual discovery. An adult penguin lay dead next to its empty nest. It was so fresh that the body hadn't frozen yet, and no signs of external injury were visible. Though mummified chick carcasses carpeted the ground throughout most of the valley, adult deaths were rare on land. Since the bird appeared to be in good shape, I decided to collect it for a museum that had requested specimens. The dead penguin was too bulky to fit inside my backpack, so I gently cradled its ten-pound body like an infant during the mile-long hike back to the hut.

"Hey, it's Thanksgiving, right?" I said, poking my head in the door forty-five minutes later.

Kirsten was busy cooking and didn't turn. "Yeah," she replied.

"I got us a bird!" I said, jokingly. We couldn't eat the penguin, of course, but I appreciated the irony.

Kirsten turned and smiled. "Hey, that one looks beautiful!" she commended. "Stick it in the freezer."

After carefully wrapping the penguin in plastic, I stored and labeled the bird for later shipment, then placed it in a cardboard box alongside bags of eggshell samples. "Someone better

159

appreciate this thing," I muttered, "since I've been carrying it for the past forty-five minutes." My stiff arms were glad to be free of the dead weight.

Thanksgiving dinner sizzled, thanks to Kirsten's industrious efforts. We had packed and saved a few special foods for the holidays, and she deftly prepared our mouth-watering meal on the small stove. Serious cooking transformed the tiny hut. Savory odors, with nowhere to escape, hung thick in the cozy, warm air.

Michelle arrived, and we tucked in to a delicious Thanksgiving dinner. Each of us ate the allotted Cornish game hen, as tasty as any industrial turkey. Kirsten had made stuffing with the precious onion. We rounded out the meal with green beans and mashed potatoes, and Michelle put together a sinfully delicious raspberry chocolate crisp dessert.

The luxury of such foods was almost too much to bear. We sat digesting long after finishing off the last crumbs.

"I'm stuffed!" Kirsten said, pushing back her chair.

"Me, too," agreed Michelle.

"That was amazing," I said, groaning a bit. "That was probably more food than I've eaten in the past week."

Kirsten laughed. "Hope it doesn't catch up with you later," she said.

160 "Hey, my system couldn't be any more fine tuned," I replied indignantly. "My digestion is perfectly disciplined."

"Good," Michelle said matter of factly, clearing our empty plates. "It's no fun to get stranded in the penguin colony."

"Yeah," I agreed. "That would never happen to me."

Famous last words.

32. Young Birders

✳✳✳

In my final year of high school, I entered a national contest called "Young Birder of the Year." The rules of the contest, organized by the American Birding Association, required keeping a field notebook, taking photographs, and crafting illustrations for seven months. At the age of eighteen, this was my last chance to qualify. After my nineteenth birthday, I would no longer be considered a "young" birder.

The previous year, I had been beaten out by a Colorado girl, who filled her notebook with incredibly lifelike paintings of gnatcatchers and flycatchers. First place in the photography division gave me little consolation. It was a good showing, but not enough. I coveted the overall title. So I labored over sketches and field notes. When packaged together with photographs and paintings from my travels, I hoped for a rock-solid contest entry. The Colorado girl had turned nineteen and disappeared into adult obscurity. The field was wide open. Now was my chance.

When judging time rolled around, I waited apprehensively. Were my materials good enough?

As it turned out, I won the grand prize. Bingo! I was the 2004 Young Birder of the Year.

A few weeks later, mountains of swag arrived in an enormous box, including a pair of expensive Leica binoculars, which would later travel with me to Antarctica and beyond. Sponsors had also kicked in stacks of birding reference books, shrink-wrapped DVDs, and software. But the best prize couldn't be contained in a package. I could choose to attend any of the ABA's young birder programs, for free. The ABA picked that year to try something new. The organization decided to hold a two-week Young Adult Birder's Conference in Ecuador. My choice was easy. This was too good to pass up.

The ABA graciously booked my tickets for the Ecuador trip
even though it was a new program. The following summer, I
touched down in Quito with high expectations. Tropical Birding,
a bird-guiding company based in the same city, would lead our
group of fifteen young adults around the country for two full
weeks. Unlike the usual gray-haired birding crowd, we college-
age birders were raring to get up early, stay out late, and go hard
all day. The tour swept us from dark depths of Amazon jungle
to chilly peaks high in the Andes. Ecuador, about the size of
Colorado, holds Earth's highest diversity of birds, and our group
wanted to see as many species as possible.

Midway through the trip, we waited on a remote, muddy
road along the country's west flank for a special bird to appear.
The rare, unusual, and nocturnal Lyre-tailed Nightjar, with tail
feathers twice as long as its body, inhabited this road cut, and we
hoped to catch it flying from a roost at dusk.

For me, the nightjar held extra portent. Standing on that
muddy road, I had seen exactly 999 species of birds in my life.
If this bird appeared, it would mark a memorable thousandth
milestone.

Keeping a cumulative list of the birds I've seen, while slightly
nerdy, is straightforward motivation. Blank spots on the list
cry out to be filled in, and the search for new birds constantly
leads to interesting, seldom-visited places, like this muddy road
in Ecuador. "Listing" also forms the basis of a little friendly
competition between birders. Occasionally, though, listing gets a
little wacky.

As darkness approached, we waited at loose ends for the
Lyre-tailed Nightjar to wake up. Suddenly, someone shouted in
excitement. "Hey, there's a Bat Falcon flying overhead!"

I groaned. I'd never seen a Bat Falcon, but the small raptor was
much more common and ordinary than a nightjar, and I didn't
want to give it the coveted thousandth spot on my life list. We
would probably see more falcons later in the trip. I made a snap
decision. "Guys, make sure to tell me when you spot another
Bat Falcon tomorrow," I said, closing my eyes and clamping my

162

hands over my ears to ignore the unwished-for new bird. "I don't want to record this one. La la la!" The falcon zipped overhead, but I didn't see or hear it. When the coast was clear, I opened my eyes, still stuck safely at 999 species.

A few minutes later, something moved on the road cut. I peered through my binoculars, trying to make out shapes in the tropical semidarkness. A wing fluttered, followed by an extremely long, loose feather. The Lyre-tailed Nightjar was waking up.

It sallied into the open, returning to the road cut to perch on an exposed piece of mud. At once ridiculous and gorgeous, evolved through countless generations of mate choice, the nightjar's twin curling tail feathers swept out behind a camouflaged brown body, wide stubby bill, and round, curious eye.

People slapped me on the back.

"Congratulations on number one thousand! That's a tenth of all the world's birds!"

"Nice one!"

"Definitely a quality milestone, man."

Nervousness prevailed until the next morning, when we eventually found another Bat Falcon in an adjacent tract of jungle. This time, I didn't block out the small raptor, appreciating instead its aerodynamic features as the predator winged and boomeranged through the sky. I cleaned up an extra life bird.

163

By the end of our trip, I had seen 517 species in two weeks, not counting a few more birds that I had only heard. Just remembering them proved a challenge, and updating my life list took hours with an Excel spreadsheet back home.

More important, I'd met fifteen like-minded bird nerds from all over North America. The world of young birders is very small, and I would bump into the same people repeatedly on future travels. Not many young people dedicate their free time to birding, but a few of them were just as loony as me.

I wasn't alone.

33. Stranded

❄❄❄

While checking nests in Area M one afternoon, a familiar feeling settled in my intestines. Then some gurgling. Pretty soon, I was doing the funny walk while navigating with my clipboard and field notebook, trying to ignore increasingly urgent missives from my stomach. The penguins must have wondered about my sudden stiff-legged gait, but I knew what it meant. Cargo needed to be unloaded, a hostage released.

I cursed my digestion. For two months, this situation had been carefully avoided through close attention to eating habits and a regular bowel schedule. So far, I'd never been stranded in the penguin colony.

"What gives?" I complained to a nearby penguin, before quickly taking it back. "I mean, no, nothing's gonna give. Crap! Wait, sh—I mean, oh, whatever …"

My gut issued some curiously loud noises that sounded a lot like the mating calls all around me. Were the birds intimidated by my stomach's territorial declarations?

I was in trouble, and I knew it.

The hut's outhouse, with its comfy foam seat and white plastic bucket, was beyond reach. I'd have to pack my gear, strap on crampons, and hike more than a mile uphill across the ice. Even running the whole way, it'd take more than half an hour, and I didn't have that kind of time. The temperature hovered around twenty below zero.

My stomach suddenly felt like a bubble holding a brick.

It wasn't my fault. In the morning, my sleeping bag had been particularly cold, so I nursed a cup of hot chocolate over breakfast. Then I ate a Hershey's bar for dessert. On my subsequent commute to the penguin colony, I ate another chocolate bar and, an hour later, merrily crunched my way through a third one—instant energy in a frozen environment. Usually, I stayed away from so much chocolate, knowing its devious qualities, but today was especially chilly.

Chocolate, of course, is loaded with caffeine. And that caffeine had my system going in top gear. Heavy artillery was now in action. Standing on the ice, surrounded by penguins, doubled over in anguish, I faced facts. It was time to make an unplanned pit stop.

Peeing in the penguin colony was permitted since liquids would eventually dissipate, warmed occasionally by sunshine on the surface. But solids were a different matter (so to speak). Organic material couldn't decompose in the subfreezing climate, and piled up instead in a semi-mummified state for eons. This was clearly evidenced by the thousands of old penguin carcasses and mounds of frozen guano scattered underfoot. Some of them had been dated to be centuries old. So there were strict rules about waste in the penguin colony. Unlike the upper slopes of Mount Everest, which are apparently littered with human turds (and bodies), Cape Crozier remained relatively pristine. Anything carted in had to be carted out.

A penguin on a nearby nest suddenly let loose with a pressurized, viscous stream of pinkish-white guano. It didn't bother to take aim, and its neighbor, sitting about three feet away 165 as the whitewash flies, was hit square in the face. The victim, for its part, didn't seem overly concerned about being used for an outhouse, and simply fluffed out its feathers while the guano slowly froze in a ridiculous spatter pattern. The decoration would be washed off on the penguin's next trip to sea.

Would that it were that easy. I definitely couldn't use a penguin for a toilet—they'd probably kick me out of Antarctica. At the moment, this was a problem. Birds carpeted the ground in every direction, densely spaced about three feet apart. Plus, making a stand in the open was chancy. Even though Michelle and Kirsten were working in distant parts of the valley, my red jacket was conspicuous.

A few hundred yards away, a snow cornice formed along a ledge over the frozen beach. It provided ideal cover, and I carefully hustled over, picking my way through the nesting penguins while trying to ruffle as few feathers as possible.

It was brisk. A slight breeze blew, the snow cornice blocked sunshine, and the temperature stung exposed skin. Shivers started running through my body and goose bumps formed around the bases of my hair follicles. A brief, ridiculous headline ran through my head: "Penguin Researcher Evacuated with Butt Frostbite." What would happen? Would they amputate?

Business taken care of, and order finally restored, I decided to leave it for a day before returning to haul it off. That would give me a chance to grab a Ziploc bag back at the hut while things froze solid. Meanwhile, the evidence would have to be buried using the only materials available: a few hardened, volcanic rocks and several equally impermeable, very frozen, long-dead penguin carcasses.

Mission accomplished, I chuckled. How many ways can you say it?

Coil some rope. Brawl with the serpent. Make a delivery. Cook a burrito. Fold in the cocoa. Lay pipe. Crack a rat. Drop off the kids at the pool. Download some software. Drop anchor. See a man about a dog. Disemfiber. Harvest horse apples. Head into surgery. Exorcise the ten-pound demon. Do a Georgia Brown. Strangle the doogler. Curl a squirrel. Get your Dijon. Visit the Chamber of Commerce. Write to the Senate. Hail Caesar. Strafe barbarians at the gate. Have a lumberjack meeting.

Free the slaves.

Sink the Titanic.

Bomb Hiroshima.

Step into the office to post a letter. The mail must go through.

34. The Chase

✳✳✳

At 4:30 a.m. I was sprinting hard down the Antarctic glacier, searching for a wily penguin to wrestle. Behind me, Mount Terror stood starkly backlit by low-angled sunlight, cracked and crevassed with glaciers and sheer cliffs. Though the sun never dipped below the horizon, it did disappear behind Terror for a couple hours around 4 a.m., and now the mountain's long, pointed shadow reached over camp, down the glacier, and past several tabular icebergs stranded offshore. Nothing moved but the wind.

Cold gusts nipped my cheeks as I hurdled snowdrifts, working downhill toward the ocean. My course tracked lines of least resistance, winding around sastrugi ridges and across patches of shiny blue ice, blown clear and polished by the last storm. Both of my quad muscles felt the effort of constant braking and swerving during the descent through treacherous inclined stretches. I balanced two steps in advance, wary of the top-heavy pack on my back. Frozen shrapnel exploded from under my crampon spikes, and each step landed with the heavy shattering sound of window panes dropped on concrete.

Somewhere ahead, a penguin waited.

I'd stayed up all night waiting for this, watching the sun gradually orbit lower in the sky. Alone inside the hut, I watched the only two movies saved on my laptop, a Pierce Brosnan caper and a Warren Miller ski flick, on repeat, all night long. Every thirty minutes, I paused the entertainment to don a pair of industrial headphones hooked up to a giant antenna mounted on the roof of the hut. If a tagged penguin returned to its nest in the colony about a mile distant, it could be heard arriving with a series of mechanical chirps from the antenna. When that happened, it was time to run like the wind.

167

Why anyone decided to put the field hut more than a mile from the penguin colony is debatable. The separation helped minimize disturbance when helicopters occasionally dropped in. But it also meant that, when a satellite-tagged penguin returned to the colony after a feeding trip, reaching it took a special kind of effort.

The chase was fun, though. Who wouldn't want to be running alone down an Antarctic glacier at 4:30 a.m., knowing that someplace ahead a penguin was waiting to be tackled?

It wasn't a hypothetical question.

I kept a good pace, carefully picking out my steps. Back in the U.S., it was 7:30 a.m. the previous day. I was running a full twenty-one hours ahead.

To be so completely off-grid, off-map, and isolated felt refreshing. I had settled in nicely to Antarctic life. My beard had grown to the point where it kept my face warmly insulated from the cold. It was also starting to make me unrecognizable. After Kirsten showed me a photo on her laptop the previous afternoon, depicting someone holding a penguin, I asked who it was. She looked quizzical, then laughed. It was me. I hardly ever looked in a mirror.

The Antarctic sky was spectacular. The sun's cool, low light—passing through layers of shimmering, extremely clear frosty air—scattered, diffracted, reflected, and refracted off ice crystals, creating a show that never seemed to repeat itself. I was glad to be wearing extra-darkened wraparound polar shades.

168

At the saddle, I stopped to quickly remove my crampons, propping them under a big rock as usual. Just a few hundred yards farther, at the edge of the massive colony, I hoped the satellite-tagged penguin would still be at its nest.

I walked this last rocky stretch, regaining my breath in anticipation of a good wrangle. The edge of the colony spread out before me with penguin nests stretching all the way to the floor of the valley. When the targeted nest came into view, however, its chicks stood alone with no parents in sight.

The penguin had gone.

In the icy chill of early morning, I stood staring despairingly at the place where the bird was supposed to be. I'd stayed up all night and run down an Antarctic glacier at an abnormal hour for nothing. Frustrating.

But the bird might still be somewhere in the vicinity. I started walking toward a portable telemetry antenna stashed nearby in case of just such a situation. If the penguin was nearby, it could be pinpointed using the antenna, which processed radio signals broadcasted from the bird's chip.

Just as I turned, my peripheral vision caught something. Several penguins were sleeping in an open space about a hundred feet downslope. They snoozed flat out on their bellies, catching a rest on a patch of bare rock. Jutting from one penguin's back were a small rectangular box and a slim antenna. Yes! It was the one I was looking for. But since it was away from its nest, it would be hard to catch. How deeply was it sleeping? Could I creep up on it?

Grabbing a long-handled net, also stashed for just such an emergency, I slowly snuck up on the napping bird. If it woke up while I was too far away to pounce, at least I could sprint after it.

The penguin must have been having fascinating dreams because it failed to wake up even when I reached under its belly to grab for its legs. As I heaved its body into my lap, the bird regained consciousness with sudden alarm. By that time I had a firm grasp on it, and efficiently removed the transmitter while the penguin tried to process what had rousted it from a peaceful sleep.

169

The deed done, I released the bird, squatted back, and breathed a sigh of relief. Every time we dispatched a satellite tag, we risked losing it. Already, one penguin had returned minus its equipment (the tape securing it had failed), and another had flat-out abandoned the colony, making an interesting nine-hundred-kilometer beeline to sea before its GPS stopped transmitting. Each tag had cost a lot—roughly $5,000—but was worth even more in groundbreaking data. Penguin behavior is naturally unpredictable, so it was with a glad heart that I successfully collected this bird's hardware.

With the transmitter safe in my pocket, I began the long uphill trudge back to the hut. It was past 5 a.m., and my tent and sleeping bag beckoned. Kirsten would take over the morning shift at 5:30. I congratulated myself on a successful mission, put one foot in front of the other, and headed for home.

35. Penguin Traffic

❄❄❄

Inspiration struck me one afternoon while I stood next to the penguin superhighway, which I'd first seen on the day I met Blackie, in a valley parallel to Area M. In this area, penguins funneled down to the valley mouth using a long, narrow strip of snow to commute between their nests and the sea.

Today, I suddenly realized something quite startling: the penguins, like American drivers and jousting knights of old, seemed to travel on the right side of oncoming traffic, passing each other with barely a glance at approaching birds. Surely, this must be random. Penguins don't have traffic laws. Why would they bother sticking to opposite lanes? But that's just what they did. They faced left shoulders to oncoming traffic. The Adélies were waddling on the right.

I pulled out my field notebook, gulped down a frozen energy bar, picked a rock in the middle of the highway as my center point, and sat down to observe. For every penguin walking uphill or downhill, I recorded whether it passed to the left or right of the rock.

It didn't take long to build a large set of observations. Penguins walked up and down the path in a thick stream. Sometimes groups backed up behind slower individuals, and some penguins slipped or collided. Several birds stalled in the middle of the road and went to sleep. Overall, though, traffic flowed pretty smoothly. During my half-hour snack break, I observed 179 individuals. About 91 percent of birds walking downhill passed the rock keeping it on their left and 95 percent of penguins waddling uphill also passed with the rock to their left (the opposite lane). The correct lane, then, was to the right!

What did the results mean? Cape Crozier is within the Ross Dependency, deeded by the United Kingdom to New Zealand,

and everyone knows New Zealanders drive on the left side of the road, as do people from the U.K. Perhaps the penguins took exception to these maniacal driving habits.

Later in the day, back at the hut, I flipped open my laptop and started surfing the Internet out of curiosity. I didn't find much about animal traffic laws, but I uncovered lots of information about the evolution of culture in humans. Could penguin behavior help link human culture and its biological past? Possibly not. Are traffic rules, then, an expression of culture in penguin society? That depends on your definition of culture, which is a slippery slope, as I recall from sleeping through my Intro to Sociology class.

I tried a different tack. Penguins may be regarded as self-automated units with the sole intention of reaching point B from point A. Like atoms in water poured into a glass, they act cohesively as a whole, but more or less randomly as individuals. Physical forces might govern their organization into opposing traffic lanes. Pedestrian dynamics comprise an entire realm of research, with complex computer models of crowds at shopping malls and cells in blood vessels. Time for another approach.

If penguins do not make individual decisions about which side of the road they prefer, they might decide as a group, like a school of fish that maintains its shape. This type of movement is called collective behavior, and we're still trying to figure it out. In flocks of flying birds, cues like vocalizations and bright flashes of white tail feathers may keep groups together. Perhaps the penguins communicate as they commute (note the Latin prefix *com-*, meaning "with"), and sort themselves accordingly.

Who can tell how a penguin's mind operates? Until we develop brainwave technology, we just won't know. Maybe, sometimes, the birds lose patience and flout the rules, resulting in a kind of penguin anarchy.

I mentioned my observations to Kirsten and Michelle.

"Nah," said Kirsten. "There's no way the penguins have traffic laws."

172

Still, I was convinced that something was up with the Superhighway. "Think of a crowded sidewalk," I said. "People form orderly lines moving in the same direction. Why not penguins?"

Much later, back at McMurdo Station, I brought up the idea with David Ainley, the senior scientist on the PenguinScience project. He calmly stroked his snowy-white mustache, casting his mind to his own observations during his years at Cape Crozier. "Yes," he said, quietly. "I've noticed that before, too. The penguins walk in strict lines, like they're keeping out of each other's way. Maybe they do stick to the right side of the road, so to speak."

If I felt vindicated, I didn't have enough data to prove it. Any kind of formal study would need a lot more observations in different places where penguins congregated. Still, until shown otherwise, I hold firm in my impression.

Penguins walk on the right side of the road.

36. Christmas

❄❄❄

December 25 was not much different from any other workday in Antarctica. Like days of the week, dates had no real significance in our life. On Christmas Day, Michelle, Kirsten, and I worked in the penguin colony like we would on any other day. We never took a day off.

But Christmas didn't pass entirely unnoticed. We celebrated the holiday by doing an official Christmas Bird Count.

The Christmas Bird Count (CBC) is an annual event in the lives of tens of thousands of North American birders, organized by the National Audubon Society. More than two thousand counts take place across the United States (and a few other places) between mid-December and early January each year. The idea is to define a circle fifteen miles wide, gather as many birders as possible, and go birding inside that circle for an entire day, keeping track of every individual bird sighted.

The annual CBC in my hometown of Eugene, Oregon, typically attracts almost three hundred birders, ranking it third among the thousands of official CBCs in terms of participation. The count is run with military precision, with dozens of different territories carved out and assigned to various teams that scout their areas ahead of time to maximize species totals. In the evening, everyone convenes in a large conference hall to thaw and dry out, eat massive amounts of home-cooked chili, swap stories from the day's outing, and pool results to try to break past count records.

Antarctica, though, had never hosted a single Christmas Bird Count—until Michelle, Kirsten, and I came along. The Crozier CBC would be a somewhat different experience with just the three of us.

It's not that Antarctica fails to qualify for a Christmas Bird Count. Yes, most of the counts are in North America. But

CBC circles also spread over Mexico, Central America, South America, and Caribbean islands. You can join counts in Hawaii, at Midway Atoll, and in Guam. There is even a ship-based count in the Drake Passage, between the tip of South America and the Antarctic Peninsula. Nobody, though, had ever completed a count on the Antarctic continent proper.

The only previous attempt at an Antarctic count had died an early death. A proposed CBC circle at Palmer Station, on the mainland south of Chile, was approved years ago but never conducted. I imagined those Palmer Station observers probably froze or succumbed to scurvy before they could lift their binoculars.

To meet the requirements of a CBC, a location must host at least one bird species that occurs in North America at other times of year. Several Antarctic birds, including South Polar Skua and Wilson's Storm-Petrel, regularly visit North American waters, easily qualifying the region for a CBC even if the penguins never waddle that far north.

I'd convinced Michelle and Kirsten that the first official Antarctic Christmas Bird Count would be worthwhile. "It's citizen science!" I expounded over a mug of hot chocolate in early December. "I mean, think about it—the first Antarctic count!"

The three of us hunkered around the propane heater, as usual. 175 "Uh, what's a Christmas Bird Count?" Michelle asked.

"My friend did one of those, once, in California," Kirsten said. "It's like you go birding all day."

"And record every individual bird," I added, cheerfully.

We stared at each other, thinking of all those penguins.

"How are we going to count every single penguin?" Michelle asked.

"Yeah, like, do we have to go around and number them all?"

"We'll do an estimate," I said.

"Estimate a quarter-million penguins?"

"Well ...," Kirsten began.

"We could ...," Michelle replied.

"Great!" I concluded, brightly. "We'll pick a day, and keep track of the birds we see in the field that day. This will be awesome!"

David Ainley approved the idea over satellite email, as did CBC compilers, even though Antarctica required a whole new section in the dataset. We agreed, in true CBC spirit, to conduct our count on Christmas Day. After all, we needed something to celebrate along with the quality chocolate we'd been jealously hoarding.

A red National Science Foundation helicopter typically makes the rounds of field camps near McMurdo Station on December 25, complete with a dressed-up Santa, but, like the Island of Lost Toys, we were too remote to be included in St. Nick's route. Cape Crozier was a little too far from McMurdo, and too risky, to warrant such a fanciful visit. The CBC would give our camp a welcome festive spark.

I hoped for three species on our count: Adélie Penguin (guaranteed), South Polar Skua (also guaranteed), and Snow Petrel (with luck). Over the previous month, we'd recorded four additional birds at Crozier, any of which were possible on count day: Emperor Penguin, Southern Fulmar, Antarctic Petrel, and Wilson's Storm-Petrel.

176 Few CBCs can rival the low species thresholds of Antarctica, but a count in Prudhoe Bay, Alaska, holds the all-time record. For the past twenty years, the annual count has tallied exactly one species: Common Raven. In 2008, the Prudhoe Bay CBC notched a particularly exciting result, posting a high tally of one hundred and nineteen individuals, though every last one was, well, a raven.

As the big day loomed, our thoughts turned to the weather. We absolutely depended on good conditions on Christmas. If a blizzard raged on Christmas, we were sunk. We'd have to delay the count, risk dangerous conditions, or record the one skua visible nesting on the helipad outside our tiny hut window.

As it happened, we worried for nothing. Christmas Day arrived bright, clear, and crisp, an auspicious beginning for our historic count.

On the morning hike to the penguin colony, we picked up
our first CBC birds. South Polar Skuas, as usual, materialized
as attack-divers, screeching and wheeling as we passed within
a hundred yards of their nests in rocky scree. One bird actually
made contact, whumping my head like a flying boxing glove.
I shook my own gloved fist in the air, but the aggressive skua
hardly took notice.

We topped out on the saddle overlooking the penguin colony
and drank in the spectacular view as we caught our breath. Rock
and ice sloped away in all directions. Every few feet, just beyond
pecking distance of its neighbor, a penguin protected its nest.
How the heck were we going to count them all? Though regular
censusing was part of our duties at Crozier, all-out population
estimates were based on meticulous office work with aerial
photographs during the off-season. We didn't have time for that
now.

As usual, Kirsten, Michelle, and I split up for the day, flipping
on our VHF radios to communicate across the wide colony.
"I'll head up Pat's Peak to do a seawatch," I said, removing my
crampons in anticipation of the rocky climb.

"All right, I'll take Area B."

"And I'll canvass the Superhighway."

"Don't worry about counting penguins," I said. "We'll do that   177
this afternoon. But anything else is fair game for the CBC, so keep
track of numbers today."

Nods of assent, and we shuffled off in separate directions, with
a peremptory "Merry Christmas!" flung over our shoulders.

After a twenty-minute hard scramble among boulders, cliffs,
and steep snowfields, I summited Pat's Peak, more than one
thousand feet above the penguin colony. The penguins below
looked like ants in the valley. I unearthed our spotting scope
stashed among the rocks, set up a clear view of the Ross Sea, and
readied for a long vigil.

Searching for movement, I swept the horizon. Against the edge
of the Ross Ice Shelf, a fin splashed in the sunlight, then another.
More than a dozen Orcas surfaced, spouting long plumes of

seawater before they submerged, hunting underneath the adjacent ice.

Something unusual appeared beyond the Orcas. A ship! It churned steadily through patchy open water and pack ice, plowing a direct path even through the thickest, most congested spots. I watched it through the scope, fascinated by the sight of outsiders on Christmas Day. Crozier was off the map in terms of navigation routes; no airplanes ever flew overhead (even at high altitudes, we never saw contrails) and ship sightings were extremely rare. Where was this one headed? It moved quickly through the pack ice, taking a parallel course to the shoreline of Ross Island, a few miles out. With my high-powered optics, the icebreaker's huge superstructure and thick-plated hull could be discerned, but the name was unreadable and nobody was visible on deck.

Then I hit the CBC jackpot. In an icy lead against the Ross Ice Shelf, two Emperor Penguins stood on a floe with shoulders hunched at the edge of open water. Their figures were easy to discern through the scope even a mile off. Pretty much all the Emperor Penguins had already gone to spend the summer among pack ice far out to sea, but, for some reason, these two lingered. They were a lucky addition to our CBC list. As I admired the Emperor Penguins, my VHF radio crackled to life.

"Better watch out, better not cry," a static-filled voice sang. "Better not pout, I'm telling you why ... Santa Claus is co-ming to town ..." Whoever it was sang the entire song, never releasing the transmit button. On my exposed perch, I had picked up the channel usually reserved for more official business transmitted from McMurdo Station.

Continuing to scope the ocean, I hoped for a Snow Petrel, and almost didn't notice when one practically whacked me over the head. Feeling a whiff of air against the back of my neck, I straightened, startled, as the petrel circled me, repeatedly gliding within five feet of the mountaintop, before winging away along a ridgeline. Its admirable pure white plumage was set off by curious black eyes. Snow Petrels have never been recorded breeding on

Ross Island. They nest in deep crevices on rugged cliffs, in places difficult to access. We encountered several such birds, indicating possible territoriality.

My radio erupted once again. Kirsten, among the penguins in Area B, reported on the line-of-sight channel. "Hey! I just had a flyby Wilson's Storm-Petrel!"

Frenzied radio discussion followed, and gesticulations. I could see Kirsten in her conspicuous Big Red parka at the floor of the valley far below, pointing into space. Having the size and flight of a swallow, the storm-petrel was too tiny to spot from my angle, but it was a very good bird for our Christmas count. "Are you eating sardines?" I asked. Storm-petrels seemed to materialize whenever someone cracked a tin of sardines, maybe attracted by the smell.

"Not this time. It just sailed by."

"All right," I said. "I'm coming down."

Quickly stashing the spotting scope, I shouldered my pack and descended into the valley of penguins.

We spent the afternoon wandering among the birds, searching for metal flipper tags. Since this was my normal daily activity, I forgot it was Christmas for most of the afternoon. As dinnertime approached, though, we reconvened and held a war conference to decide how to count the penguins. 179

"We've got satellite photos of the penguin colony," Michelle began.

"Yeah, they're clear enough to count individual birds. We could just count dots on the photo."

"Count a quarter-million dots? That'd take weeks! We've gotta eat our Christmas chocolate, remember."

"And the birds might be at a different density now than when the photo was taken earlier this season."

I thought about it. "How's this?" I said. "We conduct ground counts on a set of subcolonies this afternoon, then figure out what percentage of area they cover on the satellite photo with our GIS program. Then, we can calculate a multiplication factor to estimate the total colony population."

It sounded simple enough.

We picked a few manageable subcolonies—small, meandering hummocks densely populated with penguin nests—and counted every single penguin in those areas, ticking off individuals on handheld counters. Mentally sifting through hordes of penguins was a strain on the eyes, but much more gratifying than performing a total census.

After returning to the hut for the evening, I turned on my laptop, plugged into solar power, and analyzed the penguin colony's area with a GIS program. A few simple calculations, and our observations fueled a well-educated estimate of our penguin population. Though not an exact census, the estimate landed close to other, more in-depth studies of Crozier penguin populations. After some discussion, we decided to exclude baby penguins, which would double the overall count and inflate the perception of penguin population sizes.

And that was it for the first Cape Crozier Christmas Bird Count. We had tallied:

270,885 Adélie Penguin
79 South Polar Skua
6 Snow Petrel
2 Emperor Penguin
1 Wilson's Storm-Petrel

Reclining next to the propane heater, I broke out my holiday chocolate. "Anyone care for solid perfection?" We indulged. The bars were frozen solid and broke into dangerously pointy shards.

Michelle rummaged under a case of pots and pans, and, in a grand gesture, pulled out a bottle of fine wine, saved for the occasion. "Anyone care for liquid perfection?" We divided the wine among several mugs, unwashed from the hot chocolate.

"To the first Antarctic Christmas Bird Count—"

"And Christmas in Antarctica—"

"Hey, who's cooking Christmas dinner, anyway?"

Michelle volunteered to bake our remaining Cornish game hens, carefully packed months previously for the holidays, along with mashed potatoes and asparagus. We had split our stash of game hens evenly between Thanksgiving and Christmas. She began the work of thawing the ingredients and making space for cooking.

While she labored with the Herculean dinner over our tiny propane stove, Kirsten and I watched with appreciation, and kept conversation flowing.

"Hey, did either of you see that ship go by this afternoon?" I asked.

"Yeah," said Kirsten. "I couldn't read the name through my binoculars, though."

"Neither could I," I said, "even with the scope from Pat's Peak."

"Maybe it was the *Odin*," said Michelle, turning momentarily from the game hens, which were starting to make a deliciously oily crackle. "You know, that Swedish icebreaker."

The *Odin* breaks a shipping lane through solid ice to make way for cargo ships traveling to McMurdo Station each year. Kirsten had been on board the previous season to travel to Beaufort Island, site of another Adélie Penguin colony.

"Ah, the *Odin*," said Kirsten. "Those Swedes have it nice. That icebreaker is plush, let me tell you. Carpeted floors; a huge, beautiful wheelhouse; nice cabins; heat; fresh food ..."

Michelle and I rolled our eyes. "I'll take Cornish game hens any day," I said.

We learned later that the *Odin* was near McMurdo Station on Christmas Day, hard at work breaking ice. We had spotted a cruise ship bringing wealthy tourists to the edges of Ross Island. Most cruises in Antarctica navigate around the Antarctica Peninsula, the continent's "banana belt" south of Chile, but a few make it to the Ross Sea. This one was our closest company over Christmas.

"And just think," I said, "it's barely Christmas morning in the U.S."

While we prepared to eat our fancy dinner, everyone back home slept soundly through dark, early hours, dreaming of presents under their trees. Sometimes, I felt smug living in the future.

181

"Don't forget to send your Christmas emails," reminded Kirsten.

I hoped people at home would be tickled to receive my holiday notes from the future in Antarctica.

Though Christmas is normally a time to see friends and catch up with extended family, it was thrilling to be in the far-flung Antarctic field camp with Kirsten and Michelle. We dealt with the isolation on our own terms, never really discussing homesickness or personal matters. The three of us nurtured a solid, friendly relationship, built on a heavy work ethic and an understanding of tight living spaces. Though we encouraged communication, we kept each other's spirits up by focusing on immediate surroundings and tasks. We mostly confined thoughts of home to ourselves. Knowing that all three of us had occasional downtimes made them less worrying, even if unspoken.

I was very happy. Christmas is special, even on a typical workday. Small luxuries like Cornish game hens magnified in the harsh environment. My thoughts reached fondly to friends and family at home, waking up to Christmas morning. When I returned to the U.S., those familiar faces would be extra special. For now, I relaxed and enjoyed the holiday.

Michelle had converted our hut into a steamy, delicious-smelling chef's kitchen. "Dinner's ready!" she announced.

We stacked the game hens, mashed potatoes, and asparagus onto plastic plates, poured wine into chipped plastic mugs, and even tore off bits of paper towels to make napkins. Around the tiny table, we sat in folding metal chairs to eat our Christmas feast.

Outside, the sun shone brilliantly. It was a beautiful day. Even at the end of the Earth, Christmas had the extra glow of happiness. It was as white as could be.

Kirsten, Michelle, and I turned in early, stumbling to our sleeping tents with satiated stomachs. I picked my way into my icy sleeping bag, pulled the hood up, and fell into a contented sleep. Visions of penguins danced in my head.

37. Heat Wave

✳✳✳

January arrived with the warmest days we'd seen all season. For a few hours each afternoon, temperatures exceeded freezing, and the relative heat, at least at first, proved a nice change from bone-chilling lows of early summer. When the sun shone, the place seemed positively tropical. I stripped to two layers of fleece while working in the penguin colony, no longer preoccupied with staying warm. Hiking back up to the hut at the end of each day became a hot ordeal. One day, I removed all top layers before beginning the commute. Even with my pack cinched over a bare-chested torso, perspiration dripped.

Kirsten lifted an eyebrow as I arrived. "Lose your shirt somewhere?" she inquired.

"Just trying to stay cool," I said, out of breath. "The snow surface is becoming seriously irritating to walk on. It's got an icy crust layered over four inches of slush, half-melted by the sun, and you slide six inches on every step. Making progress is hard. Took me almost twice as long to cover the same distance."

"Yeah, I noticed that," Kirsten said. "The ice is melting everywhere."

My boots were soaking wet. "It's making rivers just beneath the surface," I complained. "Sometimes, when you break through the crust, your foot hits a pocket of icy water underneath. Hope my boots dry out by tomorrow morning."

We hadn't had a storm in weeks. Each day dawned bright and sunny with calm winds, blue skies, and Mediterranean-like climate. On some afternoons, highs reached a sweltering forty degrees Fahrenheit.

The heat wave brought a host of unanticipated problems. Our frozen dinners, meat stores, dead penguin specimens, and human waste buckets thawed out, stinking up the hut. Ice trapped inside the roof panels gradually melted, and soon every available container was deployed indoors to catch constant drips. Kirsten, in the wettest corner, worked out a complicated system of gutters and driplines to defend her bunk space from indoor precipitation. My tent, positioned outside on top of a thick snow bank, gradually sank into a five-inch-deep lake that refroze each night while I slept, setting around my sleeping pad like concrete. On my final two days at Crozier, it would take eight hours to free the tent's floor cloth from this icy foundation using an ice axe and boiling water.

The penguin colony also thawed out. "Things are going to get messy," Michelle had earlier prophesied, and I now realized what she'd meant. Snow fields on high slopes of the penguin valley issued streams of runoff that merged into a river cascading toward the beach. As it flowed through the penguin colony, the meltwater picked up heavy loads of guano, pieces of carcasses, and orange silt. The slopes seemed to drip with open, running sewers.

Everywhere was dirt, filth, excrement, and barf. Skuas picked off penguin chicks at an alarming rate, and became so overfed that they only ate the stomach contents out of each one, letting the rest of the carcass sink into half-frozen mud. Dead, gutted bodies accumulated and squelched underfoot. As temperatures rose, pungent smells in the colony became overpowering.

184

Along the beachfront, pack ice had finally dispersed enough to let some swell through, all the way from the tropical Pacific. Waves pounded a pebbled, sandy strip beneath a fantastic abutment of icicles accumulated by freezing spray. Penguins navigated these formations to dive into the still-chilly seawater, timing their moves with the waves.

Mud and flooding became serious problems in the penguin colony. Melting rivers of guano swallowed up nests that hadn't been built on high ground, and penguin chicks falling into the icy water risked hypothermia. Sopping wet baby penguins, coated in mud and filth, would huddle, shivering uncontrollably until they died.

In some places, accumulations of guano-enriched mud turned to slippery quicksand. I put my foot into several of these sumps, sometimes sinking up to my knee in thick, sandy ooze before pulling loose with a loud sucking effect.

Adult penguins seemed to hate the heat. They lay visibly panting in the sun with open beaks and fluttering throats, like huskies lounging on a hot summer day. I felt sorry for captive penguins in zoos back home. If these birds were uncomfortable in forty-degree weather, what would they think of seventy degrees?

I began to appreciate subfreezing days. Cold is challenging, but at least it is clean torture. The worst afternoons in the penguin colony were sunny, thirty-four degrees, and rancid. On one such day, I was slowly walking the beachfront, admiring an impressive display of icicles along the sandy edge as cold, heavy swells rolled into shore, when a penguin shot out of the water a foot or two away, landing close enough to shower me with spray. It was followed by a dozen more in quick succession, all of which sprinted as fast as they could up the beach, wild eyed with panic.

This was odd behavior, but I soon saw the reason for it. Just a couple yards offshore, a Leopard Seal's head surfaced like the deck of a war submarine—long snouted, gunmetal gray, flecked with black, predatory looking—and in its teeth was half a penguin. The seal had obviously done some chewing already, but it hadn't stopped thrashing the unfortunate penguin's body. It shook the bloody, feathered carcass side to side in the water, dunking it repeatedly, like a cat playing with its catch. Ribs and pink flesh, clumps of black and white feathers, appeared and disappeared behind the predator's maniacally smiling lips. This went on for several minutes until the seal submerged, taking its kill along for the ride. Just a few bloody feathers floated in the icy water, soon blown clear by the wind.

185

On New Year's Eve, Michelle, Kirsten, and I stayed up until 3 a.m. sipping cocktails and watching episodes of the television series *Horatio Hornblower* on a laptop in the hut with all the windows blacked out. It was a memorable way to enjoy the holiday, though we argued about the date. Days of the week no longer had any real significance in our lives, and none of us could remember what day it was. Estimates ranged from Wednesday to Saturday. To resolve the dispute, we had to look it up on the Internet.

New Year's Day was spent rounding up penguin chicks to index their growth. By measuring fifty randomly selected chicks, we could calculate a rough indicator of the health of the colony and compare Crozier to other colonies on Ross Island where similar indexes were taken.

Michelle, Kirsten, and I wandered around the colony on the afternoon of January 1 using a system of communication to select chicks at random.

"Got one?" asked Michelle, as we stood looking at a subcolony near Area M.

"Yep," Kirsten said, looking straight ahead. "I'm staring at a penguin chick."

"Good," Michelle said. "Go three right."

Kirsten mentally counted three chicks to the right of her randomly picked starting point. "OK," she said. "Hold on. I'm going in." She snuck up on the unsuspecting baby penguin. It was huddled in a tight group of more than a dozen medium-sized chicks that were piled together for warmth and protection while their parents went to sea. These groups, called crèches, clumped all over the valley. Kirsten reached down and grabbed the baby before it had a chance to run, cupping its chubby body between thick, soft gloves. Its friends scattered in panic to the four winds, joining other crèches nearby. "Here we go!" Kirsten said, then looked pained as the chick shot a stream of warm, thick guano all over the front of her jacket. "Aw, no, seriously?"

I laughed and placed the chick inside a soft cloth bag, suspending it from a spring scale to take its weight, while Michelle recorded the number in her field notebook. Then I removed the baby penguin from the bag to measure the length of

186

its wing before setting it gently back on the ground. It hustled to join its friends in a giant, soft huddle.

"One down," Michelle said. "Forty-nine to go!"

We took turns grabbing penguin chicks, measuring them, and recording data, each time selecting one at random via the same method, shouting "Five left!" or "One right!" after someone else picked a starting point. The larger, wilier babies could run pretty fast despite their stubby legs and tubby bodies. A "chick hook," an instrument resembling a shepherd's hook, came in handy for catching some of them. As a chick scooted away, I gently stopped it from behind, wrapping the hook around its chest just underneath the "armpits" to prevent forward motion. The baby penguins looked confused as their legs churned against the unanticipated resistance until I scooped them into my gloves.

Handling chicks was a messy business all around. The fluffy down feathers covering each bird came loose in clumps and sailed away on the breeze like gray snow. Baby penguin dandruff collected up my nose. Almost all of the chicks pooped when picked up, like rotund squeeze toys, and we learned to aim the streams away from ourselves. Even so, all of us were hit with thick, oily, fish-smelling chick guano. Outer clothing layers, unable to be washed, were forever banned from entering the hut.

By the time we'd finished, we looked like losers in a strange paintball war. Kirsten sported a long stream of dried guano across her face, from one eye to the opposite cheek. "They got us back," I said. "Those chicks didn't go down without a fight."

Handling fifty chicks was a big task, but, as the Crozier field season wound down, our biggest job lay ahead.

187

38. Bird Bums

✳✳✳

While most young adults with wildlife degrees graduate looking for a steady job, a few of us have set slightly different priorities. Not that we don't want to work—just the opposite. We seek out temporary positions paying less than minimum wage, with few days off, no vacation, no benefits, dangerous and uncomfortable conditions, grubby living arrangements, and varying isolation. Basically, we do what others don't want to, in places others can't go.

I didn't even know this was possible until midway through college, when a friend mentioned something about "bio bums" while we were out birding. "Yeah, man, it's totally feasible," he elaborated. "You can go from one seasonal job to the next, picking interesting places to visit. It's like an endless paid vacation. Great way to see the world. With your birding skills, you could land some pretty awesome gigs." He glossed over the drawbacks of such an existence—the uncertainty, the financial issues, the rigors of field work, the difficulties with relationships— and concluded, somewhat dramatically, "Few people know what's out there for someone who can put up with purposeful travel. Especially for bird folks. Among birders, it's like the birding underground."

The hub of this community is an online job site updated weekly with arcane and far-flung positions for young people interested in biology. Researchers with interesting projects often rely on motivated field techs to help with day-to-day activities. To me, it seemed perfect. People on the ground were having all the fun, anyway.

Some of the announcements bordered on the ridiculous. A quick scan of one recent installment found: "Reserve Manager,

Mindo, Ecuador. We need a creative person to steward a
50-hectare nature reserve. Provides a cost-of-living stipend, rustic
housing, and a horse."

Or: "Bird Banding Technician, Great Duck Island. Will
be stationed at a lighthouse-station-turned-field-camp with
propane lamps. Food, fuel, and fresh water delivered regularly.
Responsible 7 mornings a week. Little, if any, opportunity to
make trips to the mainland."

Or: "Research Assistant, Gough Island, Tristan da Cunha,
South Atlantic Ocean. Captive management of two bird species
and eradication of an invasive plant from steep cliffs. Extensive
experience in abseil rope-access techniques, climbing experience,
high levels of physical fitness, ability to live and work in a very
small team on one of the world's remotest islands for a prolonged
period. 13 months required."

Never mind. I was hooked on the idea. My bird bumming days
began in my gap year. I'd worked on a tropical-bird life-history
project in Panama, living next to the Panama Canal for four
months. That connection led to another field job the following
summer in Michigan with a determined crew tracking songbird
nests on a plot of land next to the historic Kellogg (of cereal
fame) mansion.

Next, I discovered Project Puffin, a long-term seabird   189
reintroduction project on several uninhabited islands off the
Maine coast. Living for a summer on different islands in tents
and an old lighthouse gave me a front-row seat for viewing
Atlantic Puffins, those clownish black-and-white seabirds with
multicolored beaks that cavort like flying feathered footballs. The
islands swarmed with Hitchcockian clouds of terns, Razorbills,
cormorants, and other iconic seabirds. Best of all, the islands were
strictly off limits to the public. We had it to ourselves.

Later that year, I found myself basking on a beach in the
Galápagos Islands, nine hundred kilometers west of Ecuador's
Pacific coastline. For three months, living with a host family
who spoke no English, I attended classes on marine biology

and received university credit. Ecology courses were held in a former resort whenever classes weren't on a beach or in a boat. The wildlife of the Galápagos, as advertised, was in-your-face: marine iguanas, sea lions, tropical fish, and, of course, the birds—Darwin's famous finches, tropicbirds with ridiculous tail streamers, stately albatrosses. Lava Herons practically had to be kicked out of the path during my commute to class. Here, I could be a student and a bird bum at the same time.

After finishing out the tennis season and my junior year in Oregon, my restless feet headed for a summer study abroad program in Fiji and Australia that featured skydiving and bungee jumping, studies on the ecology of the Great Barrier Reef and nearby wet tropical rainforests, and a boatload of birds. Imagine my ecstasy when three Minke Whales passed within feet of my snorkel mask one sunny afternoon—until I learned that celebrity crocodile hunter Steve Irwin had died by stingray strike through the heart in almost exactly the same spot. A Black Noddy, sleek, dark, and tern-like, honored his memory by alighting on my head.

Within days of my last college final, I was on a plane for Hawaii. I had loaned out my car, bought bottom-line health insurance, packed my bags, and flown to the Big Island to spend the summer working with captive endangered endemic birds in a series of high-profile aviaries on the slopes of the Kilauea Volcano. The stipend was $20 a day.

190

※

Does it take big money to finance big dreams? Not if you ask me. The beauty of a bird bum's lifestyle is lack of expenses. Willing to live simply, I have found it a near-perfect existence.

No way am I rich, but it feels rich to bum around the world for birds and avoid crummy jobs. Wherever I go, I also supplement my income by working for magazines, and keep up with editing and writing assignments via satellite Internet. Since I started freelancing at the age of fifteen, I have worked as the associate editor of *Birding* magazine, have written a regular column for *WildBird* magazine, and have sold articles and photographs to a number of other publications. I'm still not sure where these vehicles will take me, but one thing is definite: it's not a boring ride.

39. Banding

Kirsten, Michelle, and I lounged around the table in the hut, discussing the day's strategy over breakfast.

"This is it," said Michelle. "Our last major task of the field season."

Kirsten looked wistful. "Time flies," she remarked. "Seems like yesterday that all the penguins were sitting on eggs. Now we're just two days from leaving Crozier."

I plowed my way through a bowl of oatmeal, granola, frozen fruit, yogurt, powdered milk, and melted snow water, as usual, greedily spooning each bite past my drooping beard. "Yeah," I agreed, "but all those eggs have turned into penguin teenagers, and we've got to band a thousand of them! It's going to be like the Wild West out there today, penguin-style."

We were all looking forward to an action-packed day on the ice. To cap off each Crozier field season, one thousand baby penguins are marked with metal flipper bands. The banding operation had to be finished within four hours, and it was going to be tight. Fortunately, we were receiving some backup. Six people would be flown from McMurdo Station for the day to help us corral young penguins. Unfortunately, the extra labor force imposed a time limit, since a helicopter would return to pick them up at a predetermined time. We would be racing the clock.

Michelle explained how the banding would work. "We'll use that plastic fencing strapped to the outhouse," she said. "When it has been set up, the fencing forms a square about ten feet on a side. It splits into two sections at opposite corners of the square, so that teams can hold up each side, approaching a crèche of penguin chicks from opposite directions. Once chicks are in the corral, the plastic fencing can be connected to form an impenetrable enclosure."

Kirsten and I nodded, and Michelle continued. "Then the real work begins. We'll hop inside the corral, pick up a baby penguin, band it, and drop it outside the fence, then repeat the procedure. Once the enclosure is empty, we'll break it down and move on to the next penguin crèche."

"Sounds easy enough," I replied.

"Better hope you have strong thumbs," Kirsten said. "You use your thumb to manually bend the metal of each band into position around the penguin flipper. After hundreds of repetitions, we'll all be bruised and blistered."

"I always knew my thumbs were useful for something," I smiled.

After breakfast, we suited into grimy outer layers and headed outdoors. The metal bands and other supplies fit into heavy backpacks, but the penguin fence would have to be carried separately. Kirsten strapped one double ten-foot section horizontally to the top of her pack, like a set of angel wings, while I balanced the other half of the corral on top of my head for the long hike to the colony. By the time we had traversed the mile between our hut and the penguins, my body was protesting under the fence's weight. That fence seemed to grow progressively heavier until we eventually paused to rest on the last ridge. I never tired, though, of this sweeping view of the valley of penguins.

193

Today, that view was broken with an unusual sight. Six red-jacketed forms stood among the penguins—our backup from McMurdo Station, fresh off the helicopter, and fresh in general. These people had showered recently. Finding a new group of humans in "our" penguin colony was a little offputting at first. The people-to-penguin ratio was now one to thirty thousand—staggeringly crowded.

Before long, though, I appreciated their help. Among the visitors was David Ainley, who had just spent the season at Cape Royds, a relatively small Adélie colony on the other side of McMurdo Station. As the project leader, he immediately took charge of the Crozier banding operation. "Over here," he quietly directed, indicating a huddled mass of chicks in a subcolony of Area M. "We'll begin with this group of penguins."

Willing hands guided the two halves of fencing in a pincer movement, efficiently trapping twenty or thirty penguin chicks inside. When the two sides were connected, everyone hopped in to start banding.

I grabbed the nearest chick. It tried to squirm away, but was brought up short against a corner of the plastic fence, and I wrapped my gloves around its body, heaving the baby into my lap as I squatted on the ground.

It was like a blubbery, heavy, foul-smelling teddy bear with a sharp beak. The chick still retained its coat of soft, downy feathers, which, in the process of shedding, pulled loose in thick clumps and swirled on the breeze. I held the baby penguin firmly against my thighs with one hand while using the other to position a metal band around its left flipper. The material resisted stiffly while I bent it into place. Kirsten was right; after a few hundred of these, my thumbs would be bruised and battered.

The uncooperative penguin chick tried to duck out of my grasp at every opportunity. It was actually heavier than an adult penguin, with generous stores of fat and a stomach full of regurgitated fish. At last, I clipped the band into place, and hefted the baby penguin to send it on its way over the fence wall. It picked that moment to let loose with a stream of guano, straight into my face.

194

"One down, 999 to go," I said, cheerfully.

Kirsten, Michelle, Ainley, and the five volunteers were also working feverishly to band chicks inside the corral. Soon we'd blown through the initial group. We repositioned the fence around a nearby crèche to capture a new batch of recruits, and continued the process.

Time passed quickly as nine of us worked together to process baby penguins as fast as possible. I honed my routine so that I could grab a chick, band it, and release it in about thirty seconds. Some chicks were too small to band, and a few banded ones were recaptured, so activity flowed at a frenetic pace. We couldn't afford to slack off.

A couple hours later, Ainley stopped short with a baby penguin in his lap. "Anyone have any bands left?" he asked. "I'm out."

I reached into my pocket, but it was empty. The rest of our crew was likewise out of supplies.

"I think that's it!" said Michelle. "We got rid of all one thousand bands!"

It took a moment for this to sink in. Then we exchanged high fives around as we congratulated each other on a job well done.

The volunteers produced cameras and snapped a few photos of the penguin colony. We'd been so focused on getting work done that nobody had taken the time to document it. I broke out a chocolate bar and started gnawing, suddenly aware of a serious appetite.

We didn't have much time to linger, though. Distant rotor sounds warned that the helicopter had returned for its passengers. Michelle, Kirsten, and I said goodbye to the day-trippers, already making plans for our own return trip to McMurdo Station.

"We'll be there in two days," said Kirsten. "Save a spot in the cafeteria for us!"

"And don't use up all the hot water," I pleaded. "I can't wait to get a shower."

Ainley boarded the helicopter with his crew after helping to load six hundred pounds of our gear, previously stashed in the penguin colony, for the first stage of breaking camp at Crozier. "See you in a couple days," he said.

We watched the machine leave us, for the last time, alone at Cape Crozier.

40. Aftermath

❄❄❄

"It'll definitely be strange to return to civilization when this is all over," Michelle mused. "Just think of it: showers, heaters, fresh food ... what I would give for an ice cream cone!"

"You want ice cream?" said Kirsten, surprised. "We've got all the ice we can handle!"

"But no cream," Michelle pointed out.

The three of us had grown a bit rummy after two trapped days in the hut. Outside, the blizzard still raged.

I had thought about our return, many times, ever since being dropped off at Crozier months before. Time carried elastic properties in Antarctica. Sometimes it seemed to fly by, and other times it stood still. The first day was seared in memory with crystal clarity, but the subsequent weeks had merged together in the interim, and I couldn't believe the season had passed so quickly.

Kirsten picked up the list: "... cell phones, mattresses, cars ..."

"... clean hotel sheets," continued Michelle, "smelling like a whole box of bleach ..."

"Ooh, and those little containers of body lotion, with the hotel's logo imprinted," Kirsten said.

A particularly fierce gust of wind slammed the side of our hut, and conversation paused momentarily while we studied the weather display. "Ninety-two," remarked Michelle, philosophically. "That was a good one." The wind whistled through various antennas mounted on our roof and pounded the walls with flying particles of snow. Occasionally, as we ate, a rock hit the outside of the adjacent wall with a splitting crack.

"How about a warm, fluffy towel?" I said. "Or an electric toothbrush?"

"What you really need," replied Kirsten, "is a razor!" She had me there. My clean visage had morphed into a beast. The last time I shaved was the day before we helicoptered to Crozier, and my beard had flourished over its long growing season. It was out of control, actually. I refused to trim, so wild tufts of greasy hair swept from under my chin, and a rusty-blond mustache cascaded over my lip, impeding regular eating habits. Bits of food and sweat lingered from week to week since I never washed it. I could mold the growth on my face into a variety of creative animal shapes.

"None of us smells like roses," Michelle said. "With a three-month layer of penguin grime, I just hope they let us on the helicopter."

"Yeah," Kirsten added. "Can you imagine? They fly out here to pick us up, and we're covered in penguin crap. And we're standing there on the ice holding out a season's worth of human poo buckets from the outhouse, with our thumbs in the air!"

I had to agree. "If I saw myself on the side of the road, I sure wouldn't pick me up. I look like a serial killer who's been sleeping in a very cold ditch."

"At least," Michelle said, "Antarctica isn't the dirtiest place in the world. Even though we can't bathe normally, the ice doesn't stain our clothes. There's not too much mud around here besides the penguin poop."

197

Kirsten looked wistful. "Like the famous first sentence in Cherry-Garrard's book: 'Polar exploration is at once the cleanest and most isolated way of having a bad time which has been devised.' I'd say that's pretty accurate."

I cracked a grin. "Michelle, you just said 'poop' and ate a bite of spaghetti in the same breath! Society will never let us back in."

"Well, they better," Kirsten said. "I can't wait to walk into the gate at Christchurch Airport in New Zealand. The duty-free section is gonna kill me, with all those shiny, clean, well-lit displays."

"Yeah," Michelle replied. "Of course, they force you to walk through the shops on the way to the baggage claim. Temptation is hard to avoid."

"New Zealand cash is Monopoly money anyway," Kirsten said. "So it won't matter until we exchange what's left, and realize how much we spent."

At Crozier, money had lost its meaning. My wallet was stuffed in the bottom of my suitcase with my passport and travel documents, crammed in a frozen, dark corner under a bunk, where it had lain hidden for months. Over the first weeks, I often caught myself slapping at my empty pockets (devoid of phone, keys, and wallet), but the feeling of carrying civilization's necessities had worn off.

My Antarctic intern stipend was meager enough—a fraction of minimum wage—but the direct deposits from Point Reyes Bird Observatory had been accumulating quietly in my bank account. I'd saved up several thousand dollars over the season by not spending a cent.

We continued to eat, consumed by our own thoughts. Michelle, staring into space, finally spoke up. "It'll definitely be nice to see my friends again," she said.

We finished our dinner and turned in to our bunks. With the blizzard cranking outside, all three of us slept inside the hut. I stretched out my sleeping bag, hastily evacuated from my tent, on a lower bunk. Three feet above me, Kirsten bedded down in her own bunk. I could stretch out a toe and tap the hut's kitchen table while my head was pillowed against the opposing wall.

Michelle turned out the lights, so to speak, by hanging fabric curtains over the hut's two small windows. Then she crawled in to her own bunk, across from Kirsten, in soothing semi-darkness.

"Good night," murmured Kirsten.

"Sleep well," said Michelle.

I made a noise of agreement and turned over to face the wall. Six inches from my nose, the hut's south wall took the full force of the storm. Hurtling gusts of wind struck with vicious impact.

With my hand on the wood, I could feel the hut's structure vibrate under the strain.

My bunk platform was awash with loose clothing, field equipment, and other odds and ends. The space usually stored gear, and I had crawled into the pile without moving the mess. As I shifted positions, a carabiner stabbed into my back. Grimacing, I shoved the metal loop toward my feet. Sleep came hard with a freight train running past my bed, and I lay awake listening to the storm.

Soon I could hear Kirsten breathing easily above me, and Michelle slipped into the prolonged silence of slumber. Sounds of the blizzard rose and fell on the wild wind. Nothing else stirred.

My thoughts drifted. I wondered how it was possible to be so utterly happy in such an utterly inhospitable place. In the middle of nowhere, with a mega-blizzard mere inches from my face, I felt like the luckiest person on Earth.

It wasn't just the penguins that lifted my spirits. I had learned to love Antarctica itself. The remote landscape, clean and free, lacked oppressive elements, and encouraged dreams and inspiration. The daily routines were familiar and satisfying. Not once did I wake up dreading a day outdoors. Without amenities, life took on extreme focus. I received an intense sense of purpose, and began to realize that it contributed to my happiness as much as any material possession.

199

I wasn't the only one to embrace Antarctica's harsh realities. When Reinhold Messner, during his grueling ninety-two-day, twenty-eight-hundred-kilometer traverse of the continent in 1990, stopped at the South Pole Station at the trek's midpoint, the famous mountaineer-adventurer was surprisingly revolted by sudden reentry into relative civilization. Though everyone was helpful, everything "seemed unpleasant, useless, narrow and less beautiful than life in our tent," Messner later wrote in *Antarctica: Both Heaven and Hell*.

Granted, many other explorers have found Antarctica less appealing.

"Great God, this is an awful place," famously remarked Robert Scott on the day he arrived at the South Pole in January 1912, thirty-four days after Amundsen reached it. Scott's bitterness continued until his group starved to death two months later. Perhaps if they'd made it back to civilization, he would have thought more fondly of the frozen wasteland, but, by all accounts, Scott never enjoyed the expedition at all.

Ernest Shackleton's rough Antarctic voyage several years later prompted similar feelings. "If there is a hell, this is the place," quipped a member of his crew. Shackleton became a hero for bringing his men through inhuman circumstances after their ship was trapped in ice. A few years later, though, his fame subsided at home in Britain. Shackleton, restless in English society, decided eventually to return to Antarctica, but, while moored off the island of South Georgia, he dropped dead from a heart attack. On his death in 1922, Shackleton owed almost two million pounds in today's currency, lived in relative obscurity, and had been mostly forgotten until his story reemerged in the late twentieth century.

It's interesting that so many notable explorers who made it back from Antarctica died broke or unfulfilled in one way or another. Cherry-Garrard, after his near-death experience at Crozier in his early twenties, battled clinical depression for many years following his return to England. Even Admiral Richard Byrd, one of the most distinguished American Antarctic explorers, saw his role downplayed by the U.S. Navy as he grew old in the 1940s, which, according to one biographer, "contributed to his failing health and eventual death."

Antarctica seems to put an icy grip on anyone who ventures there. Faced with its stark contrasts, people deeply experience the thin, thrilling divide between life and death. "It's the only place in the world where I feel part of something bigger than life itself," a worker on our McMurdo Station safety crew said.

For me, Antarctica marked a beginning. But it was only a temporary home. As I fell into sleep, my thoughts were carried by the wind to the true residents of Antarctica, those curious, fearless, mischievous, and competent Adélie Penguins marching inexorably forward into the cold.

Acknowledgments

I am deeply indebted to David Ainley for his help and advice in my fledgling efforts as an avian researcher, writer, and photographer. His thoughtful comments in reviewing this book were invaluable. His knowledge of penguins, and his quiet, constant passion for penguin research, are nothing short of inspirational.

For a wickedly awesome field season with Adélie Penguins in Antarctica, I am grateful to Michelle Hester and Kirsten Lindquist of the Cape Crozier field crew, and to Grant Ballard and Katie Dugger of the PenguinScience research team.

Thanks to Bruce Dugger, Ted Floyd, Geoffrey Hill, Rose Borzik, and Douglas Robinson for their strong support of my Adélie Penguin Population Ecology Internship application.

Also thanks to the National Science Foundation, Office of Polar Programs, for funding the PenguinScience research project (NSF grant 0440643), and the U.S. Antarctic Program for supplying all the logistics, tents, and food involved. I acknowledge the folks at H. T. Harvey & Associates, PRBO Conservation Science, and Oregon State University who designed and are carrying out this project.

Mary Elizabeth Braun, Acquisitions Editor, and Jo Alexander, Managing Editor, at Oregon State University Press, have been the best editors a young author could ever hope for. I also appreciate the able assistance of Associate Director Tom Booth and Editorial & Marketing Associate Micki Reaman at OSU Press. I am grateful to David Drummond for the crisp book cover design and to Grace Gardner for the great maps.

I thank the anonymous reviewer whose comments helped make this a better book.

Finally, I wouldn't be here without such great parents, Lisa Strycker and Bob Keefer. Their support and encouragement have literally meant the world to me, to the end and back.

Index

❋

205

207